To dr. *[illegible]*
with compliments from:
[signature illegible]

———————————

Pretoria, South Africa
Sept. 1960.

THEIR SECRET
WAYS

THEIR

BUSHVELD
STORIES BY

ILLUSTRATIONS

SECRET WAYS

VICTOR POHL

FRANCOIS KRIGE

OXFORD
UNIVERSITY
PRESS

LONDON · CAPE TOWN · 1960

Oxford University Press, Amen House, London E.C.4

GLASGOW   NEW YORK   TORONTO   MELBOURNE   WELLINGTON
BOMBAY   CALCUTTA   MADRAS   KARACHI   KUALA LUMPUR
CAPE TOWN   IBADAN   NAIROBI   ACCRA

PRINTED BY THE STANDARD PRESS LIMITED, 34 GLYNN STREET
CAPE TOWN

B1746 OH

DEDICATION

To my brother Eric
and everybody who knew Dassie

AUTHOR'S FOREWORD

The stories and sketches in this book, though they are all concerned with my experiences and adventures with animals, fall naturally into three divisions. There are first the adventures of my childhood on a farm on the Basutoland border of the Orange Free State, where wild life was still almost untouched. Later adventures with gun and fishing rod follow, and some account of the strange ways of animals that I have myself observed. And last there is the story of Dassie, the dog whose companionship meant more to me than that of any dog I have owned.

In reading over the story of Dassie, it occurred to me that only those who love and know dogs can credit the unusual qualities that some of them display; and I might have felt it necessary to keep on assuring my readers that this is a true story, were it not that so many people, including heads of police, journalists and others too numerous to mention, both in my home town of Bloemfontein and in other parts of South Africa, knew Dassie well, and know that these things really happened.

ACKNOWLEDGEMENTS

MY THANKS are due to Mrs. Charles Elginton whose insistence led to the writing of my adventures with animals; to Dr. A. C. Hoffman of the National Museum at Bloemfontein for much valued assistance; and to Mrs. N. J. Marquard for encouragement, advice and help in the writing.

CONTENTS

Part One

CHILDHOOD ON THE BASUTOLAND BORDER

Part Two

A DIVERSITY OF CREATURES

Part Three

DASSIE

THEIR SECRET WAYS

Part One

CHILDHOOD ON THE BASUTOLAND BORDER

Introduction

MY INTEREST in the creatures round about me began so far back that the sight of two ants pulling a fly in opposite directions seems to be one of my earliest memories.

A little later I remember arousing my sister Adriana's displeasure because I could not, or would not, understand a sum. At the end of the lesson I wandered off to the foot of a near-by koppie, and sat down gloomily on a stone to brood on my hard lot and on the futility of having one's mind stuffed with unnecessary facts. Presently a soft noise, a kind of sighing in the grass, attracted my attention. It was caused by hundreds of termites busily carrying grass to their nest.

The classroom with its windows facing the distant Maluti Mountains was instantly forgotten, and soon I was absorbed in breaking up grass stems into lengths and placing them close to the ants' holes, immensely pleased at lending a helping hand.

Imagine my surprise and disappointment when some of the termites, after a cursory inspection, deliberately removed

2

my pile out of the way, as if to say, 'No good to us.' I could no more understand this ungraciousness than I could the reason for doing sums.

On my way home I saw a movement in a small mound of freshly dug up earth. I knew it was made by a mole, and I thought he might be trying to let in some fresh air, so I promptly went to his assistance, removed the mound, and opened up the hole before I sat down on a convenient ant-heap to watch for his return. In a minute or two the opening was suddenly filled again, not with the mole but with a small new mound! I could not at all understand why anything should prefer to live in a dark, dank dungeon when there was so much loveliness and sunshine outside.

The events of that afternoon were the beginning of a life-long interest, which became almost an obsession, in the habits of all wild creatures. I had other interests, and it was music that later became my profession, so I did not have the time, nor in fact the inclination, to make a scientific study of insects or animals; but I watched with never-failing interest the ways and peculiarities of all creatures with which I came into contact.

Few people not born and bred in South Africa have written authoritatively about its animals and plants. One of these was

J. Guille Millais, who travelled by ox-wagon from the Cape to the northern Transvaal by slow stages in 1898, and was able at his leisure to put his impressions on canvas, and write interestingly and accurately of what he had seen and experienced on the way. But after a long life of close contact with the soil of my native land, I am still frequently intrigued and surprised by the behaviour of some of the denizens of veld, vlei, and river that I had imagined I knew all about. Millais found, as many have done since, that the nature of the soil and the wild life it supported changed at almost every trek with bewildering variety, and felt that long years of experience alone would enable him to get a clearer picture of a world so diversified.

But the picture is changing with the encroachments of civilization. In the Orange Free State, where there is little bush cover in the flat open country, the larger animals have been wiped out, and it is surprising that so many of the smaller types of animals, and some species of birds, have managed to survive.

The nightmare-bird, that will-o'-the-wisp of the vleis with the ghost voice, has almost disappeared, and so, at least in the flat, grassy parts of the province, has the lynx. The former has vanished because the vleis in which it lived have been rapidly drying up in the face of farming and cultivation, and the lynx, skilful as it is in stalking its prey, has not been able to guard itself against almost complete extermination by the white man.

There is little doubt that the three kinds of hare found here will, thanks to their prolific breeding habits and powers of running, easily hold their own, even though only a minimum of grass and scrub remains for cover. But waterfowl of every kind will find it increasingly difficult to survive because of the want of open water and vleis.

I was fortunate in growing up in the comparatively untouched country on the banks of the Caledon River, and in having opportunities of observing animals now possible to few in our increasingly urban life.

4

🌿 *Hammerheads* 🌿

THE MOST VIVID of my early memories are those of wild birds: *kiewietjies,* or plovers, in the open patches near the homestead, swallows flying under and diving from the eaves before the first rays of the sun had crept through my open window, and hammerheads screaming harshly from the kranses that edged the hills a hundred yards from our front door.

The kiewietjies were always there, winter and summer, ready to protest at the tops of their voices should man, dog, cat or meerkat come near them; and the soft familiar half-whine of the swallows coming and going from the eaves as the sun came over the Maluti Mountains, will always linger as one of my loveliest memories of the past. But the peculiar habits of the hammerheads were so intriguing that their weird rasping calls never failed to arrest my attention, and, even after the novelty had worn off, my interest remained.

In about 1895 we trekked to a farm called Alpha, near the banks of the Caledon River, which forms the boundary between the Orange Free State and Basutoland, and after the flat farm on which we had lived on the western plains of the Free State, we found our new and beautiful surroundings, with the great barrier of the Maluti Mountains to the east, very exciting.

The morning after we arrived my brother Eric and I, aged about seven and nine, were out early to explore. Suddenly we saw a drab-looking bird about as big as a crow sailing majestically over the rantjie, or hilly ridge, on which our house stood. At the edge of an overhanging krans there was a mound of debris that looked as if it had been washed up by a high tide. The bird flew to this and settled on it, with something dangling from its beak. The beauties of the landscape were promptly forgotten and we made for the spot, keeping out of sight behind the kraal wall, until we were about twenty-five

yards from the mound, but by this time the bird had disappeared.

We started to climb up the ridge, to find out what it had been carrying; but a deep kloof prevented us from reaching the mound. We made our way down by a footpath, and we could plainly see a collection of sticks and grass projecting well out over the edge of the rocks. Then we tried to climb each flank of the krans in turn, but found them unscalable.

We were just about to go away when we saw the bird coming from the vlei and again carrying something in its beak. It settled on top of the mound, dropped its burden, which looked from where we stood uncommonly like a frog, and gave a succession of piercing screams. Then it picked up the frog again, stepped over the heap of sticks, swung upside down on a twig, and in a flash disappeared into the rubble. Crane our necks as we would, we could not see the hole by which it had entered.

At that time a Basuto boy of about eighteen, named Lehaoa, was working for us. Lehaoa was a great sportsman; he could hold his own against all comers at throwing sticks, and he had the reputation of being a formidable fighter. We boys never had a better friend. Now on our way home we met Lehaoa going to the fountain and told him about the hammerhead nest, and pointed it out to him. He at once agreed to help us reach it, but said that he would not as much as touch a stick or straw of it. We were surprised at this, but after he had assured us that if you kill a hammerhead you will certainly be struck by lightning, we began to have grave doubts about the wisdom of carrying out our project.

As soon as we reached home we told Father what Lehaoa had said, and asked if it was true. My parents always took the trouble to explain things that puzzled us, clearing away our superstitious fears, and now it did not take Father long to discredit the hammerhead–lightning theory. But he explained that although the Basutos were perhaps no more superstitious than Europeans, their own peculiar beliefs were so deeply ingrained that it would be useless for us to try to convert Lehaoa to our way of thinking.

As soon as he had finished his work, Lehaoa accompanied us to the nest as he had promised. With a few strong poles he made a bridge for us to cross the ravine that divided the hammerhead's rock from the main krans.

We imagined that it would now be a simple matter to rob the nest of its eggs or fledglings, but we were soon disillusioned. The nest was conical in shape, about four feet in diameter, and three feet in height, and it was almost as hard as the rock itself. It was impossible to break it open, and if we wanted to get to the entrance, we would have to let ourselves down the face of the krans. Eric and I were of course much too scared to attempt anything of the sort, and as Lehaoa's scruples forbade his giving us any further help, he suggested that we should get Jafta, a Bushman who had been with the family ever since we could remember, to help us.

When we told him of Lehaoa's superstition about hammerheads

Jafta raised himself to his full four foot seven inches, snorted, and expressed his scorn of Basutos in general. Then he continued, 'I never kill hammerhead, he too thin and stinks too much. But if your want his chickens I take them out for you. Basutos! Bah!'—and he spat through the window. Jafta was of course well aware that Lehaoa held exactly the same opinion of Bushmen.

We were delighted at Jafta's promise, and a few days later we set off again. Jafta secured one end of our rickety bridge to some projecting rocks on top of the krans, and tied a strong ox-riem or thong, to the other. He then let himself down a few feet till he found a footing on a small ledge below the nest. Standing on this he could insert his arm into the entrance passage, and he found that it first sloped upwards and then curved inwards towards a kind of chamber.

Stretching up as far as he could, he just managed to touch with the tips of his fingers a soft object, and at the same moment he felt something wet and warm swishing up against his hand and arm. For a moment he thought that he had been spat at by a cobra inside the nest; but the next moment a most horrible smell reached his nostrils, and he found that his hand and arm had been sprayed with the excreta of one of the young birds, its instinctive method of defending itself. Luckily for Jafta there was rain-water in one of the many hollows in the rocks near by, and he lost no time in washing his arm thoroughly.

He felt so humiliated by his misadventure that he wanted then and there to attack and destroy nest and inmates alike; but finding that he might as well attempt to uproot a hill with his bare hands, he decided to run home for a pitchfork, for he was determined to see what it was that had besmirched him. It was only after half an hour's hard work with the pitchfork that he at last succeeded in demolishing the nest. By then his probing with the pitchfork had killed the young birds, which were almost fully grown, and our hopes of securing them alive were disappointed.

While Jafta was breaking up the nest, we noticed a great

variety of oddments adorning its top—bits of tin, bones, pieces of skin and leather, the skeletons of several small birds, and a host of other things; and when we discovered a rusty table-fork we at once became so interested that we decided to make a thorough search of every nest that we could reach. A couple of days later we found on top of one nest a leather purse so bleached and cracked by sun and wind and rain that it was barely recognizable, but it still contained some small change in silver. Father felt sure it had once belonged to one of the many Basutos crossing the Caledon River on their way to and from Johannesburg.

This find so excited us that we went farther afield, over the boundary into Duncan's farm, to look for more treasure; but the only excitement we got was to be unmercifully stung by a colony of bees that had made their home in an abandoned nest in the fork of a willow, and only the presence of mind of Jafta, who hurriedly led us through a thick patch of trees, saved us from worse injury.

At this time Eric and I were too young to take an intelligent interest in the habits of the hammerhead, but much later I realized that the reason why this bird never makes the slightest attempt to conceal its home is because it learned, long before man came on to the scene, to place it so cunningly and construct it so stoutly that its enemies were unable to destroy or rob it; not even a baboon, however strong, clever, and destructive it may be, can make an impression on it. Indeed, the hammerhead's jaunty walk and supremely confident air, and the clear penetrating scream it gives even when perched on top of its house, appear little less than a challenge to all to dare rob its nest.

Once when I was recuperating from an illness, I wandered to the river and lay down under a drooping willow at the edge of the clear stream. The chattering and chirping of birds in the tree overhead and the murmuring of the stream sent me to sleep.

9

Suddenly I was awakened by a harsh scream close at hand, and on opening my eyes I found the disturber of the peace to be a hammerhead wading in the water not more than five yards from me. It was quite unaware of my presence, and I was well screened by the trailing branches of the willow. The stream at this spot was from six inches to a foot in depth and crystal-clear, and I was able to observe the bird's every movement right down to its straggling toes, and its crested head and straight, sharp beak seemed only a few feet away.

There were many small patches of partly submerged water-weeds in the stream, and each of these he visited in turn. He would move towards a patch very stealthily, then insert a foot into the weeds and shake it vigorously, whereupon the inmates would dash out for safety, only to be transfixed by the sharp beak hovering over them. After gobbling up numerous tadpoles, he roused a large frog which he killed with one thrust of his beak, and then he sailed away with his trophy to his nest. On his way back he called his mate, 'Krank, krank, krrrrr krank krank', and when the latter arrived on the scene she received as enthusiastic a welcome as might have satisfied the queen of birds. Flapping his wings, screaming shrilly, wheeling, capering delightedly, he made a commotion that might have caused every frog in the river to dive for safety. The hunt, however, was soon on again for food to satisfy the ever-growing appetites of the young birds, and it continued till dusk, when I could hear the homing cry of the male coming from the direction of the nest, and then only was there an end to the day's hard work.

We were often hard put to it to catch sufficient frogs to bait our night lines with, and now that we had discovered that the hammerheads were responsible for the shortage, Stefans, our eldest brother, swore that he would shoot on sight any hammerhead that came within range of the old muzzle-loader. This proved to be no vain threat, and soon there were very few left to carry on their nefarious occupations on the vleis close to the homestead. But one day, as one was flying past him in the river, Stefans took a shot at it without doing any damage beyond detaching a few feathers that came spiralling down on to the stream. Three Basutos who were watering their horses on the far side of the river saw the incident, and, gesticulating wildly they jumped on to their animals and forded the river, which was very low. Coming up to us, they dropped from their horses, breathless with haste and perturbation, and could hardly talk fast enough in their efforts to convince Stefans of the folly of his action, and to congratulate him on the bird's escape.

We were on friendly terms with the Basutos from over the border, and they felt it their bounden duty to warn Stefans of the terrible fate that would have befallen him had his bullet found its mark. There was not the slightest doubt in their minds that had he killed the bird he would have been struck by lightning the very first time a storm came up. Some Basutos, indeed, are so alarmed if a hammerhead flies over their huts uttering its raucous cries, that they will abandon them and build elsewhere for fear of misfortune.

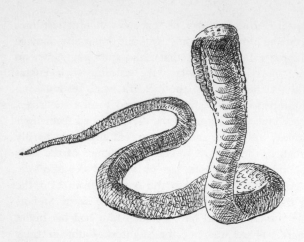

Mostly cobras

JUST ACROSS the Caledon River lay Basutoland, the river forming the boundary line between it and the Orange Free State. The farms on the Free State side were widely scattered, and our farmhouse was situated on a rantjie, or flat ridge, that overlooked the river about 250 yards away.

On the Basutoland side of the Caledon, the Maluti Mountains rose into an intense blue sky, and the country on both sides was a never-ending source of delight and interest to us. When we knew it, the larger antelopes that had once roamed there had disappeared, as had the lions that preyed on them, driven by the bands of Basuto hunters to safer feeding-grounds. Only small herds of springbok, steenbok, and *rooi* (red) or *vaal* (grey) rhebok were left. But there was still an abundance of game-birds, especially water-fowl, and of fish; and, unfortunately for us, of snakes there were apparently as many as before the Voortrekkers came.

A very common snake at one time was the water-snake, but it has become almost extinct as the vleis and pans in which it lived have disappeared. Water-snakes grow to about three

feet, are slate-coloured on top, and pale yellow under the belly. They are comparatively slow in their movements and, being of the back-fanged type, were for long supposed to be non-poisonous. In fact during the winter months, when they roll themselves into compact balls inside the water-weeds and grasses, we boys often handled them as if they were so many oranges and shied them at each other in fun.

My most vivid recollection of a water-snake goes back to a time when Eric and I were looking along the banks of the river for frogs to use as bait. I was walking at the water's edge and Eric was higher up on the bank, when a frog which he had disturbed made a prodigious leap towards the river. Had all gone well it would just about have reached the water; but as it was sailing over a patch of grass about two yards from the stream, something shot out towards it, and the frog disappeared so suddenly that Eric and I gasped in astonishment. On coming nearer, we saw a water-snake holding the frog in its jaws.

Our parents' constant fear was that Eric and I might encounter poisonous snakes, as they had been warned of the very large number in the vicinity. That these fears were not groundless was proved during the second week after our arrival.

I was taking a stroll by myself along the rantjie, enjoying myself and at peace with the world. A typical summer thunderstorm had passed over the farm the previous day, and there were puddles of water everywhere; but the skies had cleared and a steamy heat filled the air—ideal weather for snakes to sun themselves or to lie in wait for possible victims. I was a few hundred yards from home when I climbed a slanting rock and sat down to watch the countryside. Presently, about fifty yards away, I saw a *koggelmander* (large lizard), about a foot long, lifting itself on its forearms and subsiding in a quick succession of ups and downs, a sign that it had seen something suspicious. As human beings fall into this category I thought it was trying to frighten me, but as it was perfectly harmless I was merely interested.

The stone on which it was sunning itself stood out about a foot above the surrounding grass. Suddenly I saw a movement, but it was too swift to follow, and the next second the lizard disappeared as if by magic. Thoroughly interested, I walked to the spot to see what had become of it, my eyes fixed on the stone, expecting to see it hiding in one of the cracks, when I trod on a yielding body, and at the same instant I felt something strike against my leg. Instinctively I jumped away, and about two feet from me I saw what seemed to me an enormous snake lifting itself and extending its hood. I got such a shock that I remembered nothing of my flight to the house; I only remember that a little later I returned to the place with Stefans, but when we got to within twenty yards of it I could not be persuaded to go another step. Stefans was rather sceptical about the whole affair, but when he found a koggelmander lying dead exactly where I said the snake had been, he told me to remain where I was while he looked around.

Hero, our nine-month-old mongrel dog (of whom I shall have more to tell later), had followed us, and after he had nosed around he went straight towards a small clump of thick grass about twenty yards away. Stefans thought it unlikely that at his age Hero would follow up the spoor of a snake, and supposed at first that he had scented a hare or a partridge; but as the dog circled round the patch sniffing suspiciously and bristling all over he followed him to find out what he was after. Presently Hero came round to my side of the patch and suddenly, not more than a yard away from him, a large cobra raised itself to a height of about three feet, with hood extended and tongue flickering. Stefans's first reaction was to prevent the dog from getting within range of the snake's fangs, for although all dogs have an instinctive fear of snakes it is only the older and more experienced ones that are sufficiently intelligent to keep out of harm's way. But Hero mistook Stefans's coming towards him as a sign that he should attack the snake.

The cobra struck as soon as the dog came within reach, and buried its fangs in his neck for a fraction of a second before he shook it off; and at almost the same moment Stefans's stick caught it in the middle, and a few heavy blows ended its career.

We ran home as fast as we could to see what could be done for the dog. Father examined the wound and, to our great relief, said that the fangs had entered the skin obliquely, and that he was sure that only a very small amount of poison had got into the bloodstream, especially as Hero's skin was unusually loose and thick. In spite of this, however, the dog was at death's door for two or three days. His head and neck swelled to an enormous size; he hardly moved all that time, and it was with great difficulty that we forced milk down his throat.

Meanwhile we went back and retrieved the cobra as well as

the koggelmander it had killed, and then I realized how narrowly I had escaped. Had the snake not been holding the lizard in its jaws when I stepped on it, I should certainly have been bitten.

On most of our adventures we were accompanied by our dog Hero. He was about as heavy as a bull-terrier, but longer in the legs. He was the most fearless and faithful creature I had known, and was hunter, watchdog, playmate, and fighter along with us.

A week after the adventure with the cobra, Father killed a young puff-adder some distance from the house and brought it home for us to see. Hero sidled up to it cautiously, every hair bristling. He circled slowly round the snake, facing it all the time, his neck stretched to its limit, and sniffed at the body with his nose nearly touching it. He had learned his lesson, however, and at the slightest movement he would jump back a couple of yards. But gradually he closed in and then all of a sudden he grabbed the adder and hurled it yards away from him, only to start sparring once more. Leaving him to this game, we all went indoors for a cup of coffee, and when we emerged again the pup was busy cracking every bone in the snake's body. He had started from the tail, and was crushing it with his teeth along its entire length, till it must have been obvious, even to him, that it was dead.

Since those days Eric and I have had a great deal of experience of snakes but nowhere else have I seen as many as on the banks of the Caledon. Everything was in their favour. They could shelter in crevices in the rocks of the ridges running parallel to the river, in ant-bear and spring-hare holes, in the long thick grass, and in the many hollow tree-stumps that had been washed out on the banks when the river was in flood. There were countless small birds, mice, rats, frogs, and toads for them to live on. And, moreover, in this happy hunting-ground I never saw a Basuto kill a snake, though we never discovered the reason for this.

One of our favourite pastimes was to hunt for small or

immature snakes under the flat stones that were strewn all about the rantjies, often only two or three inches thick, the hollows under them affording excellent cover for small snakes of every kind.

I have excellent reason for remembering our first hunt of this kind. We had already killed several smallish snakes, and I was in the act of forcing my hand under a stone in order to lift it, when an excruciating pain shot through my hand and arm. We were about a hundred yards from home, and I made tracks for it as fast as my legs could carry me.

Luckily, Father was at home, and when I told him what had happened, he ran to the spot, and Eric pointed out the stone I had tried to lift. He prized it up, and beneath it he found a large brown scorpion.

He was very much relieved when he found that I had not been bitten by a snake; and my own fears were set at rest and even the severe pain I had to endure for several days did not prevent me from joining in the same kind of hunt again, though we were a little more cautious after that. Actually, whenever a snake was suddenly uncovered, it was blinded by the sunlight, and this made the sport much less dangerous than it might otherwise have been.

A year is a long time in the life of a small boy, and still longer in that of a young dog, and at the end of a year at Alpha, Hero, Eric, and I regarded ourselves as decidedly expert in veld lore. To be sure, we had had some narrow escapes; but such incidents did not dampen our spirits or diminish our zest for out-of-door adventures. On the contrary we found our hours of schooling under my mother and my sister Adriana drag more than before.

There were far more cobras than any other kind of snake on our farm, and Father put this down to the fact that cobras are inveterate killers of other snakes. So, one way and another we were always encountering these bad-tempered hooded reptiles, almost to the exclusion of puff-adders, yellow cobras, and night-adders.

One afternoon Hero, Eric, and I, accompanied by the Duncan boy and his dog Vuilbaard, sallied forth to hunt the quails that were to be found in the grass patches bordering the corn-lands. Both the dogs had often succeeded in scenting and pouncing on quails before they could take to flight.

Hero was in the habit of going some yards ahead of us, and never failed to warn us if there was a snake in our line of march, and on this afternoon we were walking in single file with Hero and Vuilbaard a little in advance of us, when Hero bristled, stopped, and then started circling round a spot about five yards ahead of us.

Suddenly a large cobra raised itself well above the grass with hood threateningly extended. Hero had by now become such an expert killer of snakes, and we had such complete confidence in him, that we merely waited for him to deal with the cobra, sure from our experience that its fate was sealed. As usual, he started slowly circling round it in order to tire it and make it dizzy, just as a mongoose or other snake-killer will do. But we had forgotten about Vuilbaard, who knew little about snakes. At first he kept his distance, but incautiously he came within striking distance, and the cobra struck him between nose and eye. He whimpered and jumped away, but not before the cobra had had time to inject a full dose of poison.

Rushing in while the cobra's attention was distracted, Hero seized it in the middle and shook it so violently that it broke in two. To Eric's consternation the front part landed with a thud on his chest, and then fell to his bare feet; at the same time a long string of entrails was splashed on to his cheek and ear.

For the moment we had forgotten Vuilbaard, but almost at once, as we turned to attend to him, his back started sagging, and foam formed on his chops; and in less than ten minutes he was stone-dead.

For a combination of daring, coolness, and quickness of movement, I doubt whether there is any animal in South Africa to equal the *vaal muishond*, or South African grey mongoose. There are various kinds of mongoose, differing in size and colour, but they are all alike in build and character. Not only are they fearless fighters, but they will eat any creature they can beat, whether insect, bird, reptile, or small four-footed animal.

I once witnessed a fight between a vaal muishond and a large black cobra. Eric and I had just been promoted to the use of the old shotgun. We had noticed that a number of spur-winged geese were in the habit of settling in the vlei below the rantjie just before sunset every evening. Owing to the weight of our weapon we had not yet learned to bring down birds in flight, so we decided to erect a hide-out beneath an overhanging rock half way up the rantjie and about twenty-five yards from the water's edge, covering up the opening with a few leafy branches.

We were so keen to forestall the spur-wings that we were in our hiding-place at least an hour before sunset. While we were waiting, we saw a vaal muishond coming along the edge of the vlei towards us. He would stop every now and then to have a good look round and then advance again fairly rapidly; but as he was coming round a sharp bend about sixty yards from our hide-out, he suddenly dropped his nose to the ground, and seemed to have scented something particularly interesting. He followed the trail as a pointer might have done, till, just opposite to us, he stopped and half-circled a dense patch of grass. He then dived into it, and as he disappeared, one of the largest brown cobras I have ever seen reared itself from cover and stood towering over the puny little fellow.

Eric was so excited that it was all I could do to prevent him from jumping out from behind our screen; but what had really prevented me from doing so myself was the sight of a spur-wing circling the vlei as he called to his mates in husky 'sewaaks'. For a brief second our eyes followed the heavy bird, till it settled well out of range of our shotgun; but when a moment later we turned towards the ill-matched pair below us, we were more than surprised to see the muishond dashing around the snake much as Hero always did when he was sparring for an opening. We did not think for a moment that the little creature had any chance against his huge and dangerous opponent, and we fully expected to see the snake bite and paralyze him. But it was soon evident that the muishond had no intention of retiring. On the contrary, he never gave the snake a moment's rest, but kept dashing in and out, and circling round it, forcing it to remain upright.

The muishond was of course 'our man', and we were prepared to back him to the last ditch, but his methods appeared to be suicidally reckless. He would come up so close to the snake that he had to look straight up to see the flickering tongue and menacing hood, and every time the cobra lunged he seemed to escape death by a hair's breadth. That impudent little face, almost rubbing noses with the cobra, was an astonishing sight. We were drawing mental comparisions between his methods and Hero's, but this little chap was far more heavily handicapped than the dog ever was, for while Hero could 'ride' the lunges, as it were, by merely turning sideways, or leaning backwards, this midget had to remove himself completely to get out of harm's way.

It was evident that part of his plan was to tire the snake, for every time the snake struck and missed meant so much loss of energy. And after some time we could see that the snake was finding it increasingly difficult to rear after it had missed its mark, and Eric kept repeating under his breath, 'Courage, little mongoose'. Then it was not long before the cobra was so tired that it could hardly lift itself; and as its head touched ground after a final feeble stroke, the mongoose flashed in with astonishing rapidity, caught it behind the head, and mauled it till even we could see that it was dead.

We were so excited and so filled with admiration for the small fighter that before we realized it Eric and I had leapt out of the hide-out, whereupon the mongoose took to his heels, and the spur-wing circled out of range. We left the snake where it lay;

but passing that way the next morning we found that it had disappeared, and we hoped fervently that its conquerer had made a meal of it.

One warm, dark night we heard a commotion in the fowl-run. Father immediately seized the shotgun while Stefans took the lantern. This gave only a poor light, so they kept a good look-out and approached the run very carefully. In front of one of the nests they found a hen lying dead, and Father was bending down to examine it, when Stefans shouted a warning. He shifted the light slightly and they saw a cobra reared up, ready to strike or spit. Before Father could move away, it spat in his eyes. He was almost blind with the pain of it, and Stefans had to help him to get back to the house. When Mother realized what had happened, she washed his eyes with milk, a recognized specific against the blindness that may be caused temporarily, and sometimes permanently, by the spit of a snake.

Looking back at the many adventures we had with cobras, I have come to the conclusion that cobras are more dangerous, and have caused more deaths in South Africa, than even the dreaded mamba. Not only are they far more numerous, but, in summer at least, they are almost as active at night as during the day. The mamba is extremely vigilant and easily alarmed, but except in the mating season it will only strike at something that bars its way, while the cobra when it feels itself threatened will always attack to defend itself. On the other hand, I have often found that, even though apparently aggressive, a cobra will slip away when it finds that it is unobserved; and by the time I have turned to look for a stone to throw at it, I have come back to find that it has disappeared. I would never strike at a cobra with a stick for fear of receiving a charge of poison in the eyes. Like most animals, it is most dangerous when cornered, and although it only strikes the length of its body, its lunge is as swift as lightning.

We meet the herdboys

OUR FIRST summer had passed, autumn had given place to midwinter, and the Caledon, fed by the snows of the Malutis, was crystal-clear and icy-cold; and the piercing south-wind that moaned in the keyhole of our rondavel door, often filled me with a youthful sadness that only sleep or the comfort and warmth of a good fire could dispel.

Far and near, roll-bushes driven by the wind careered madly over the veld, to be caught in a fence or to fill hollows and furrows to overflowing and make snug cover for the smaller creatures of the veld. They were the dried skeletons of bushes that flourished everywhere in the lands, growing to a height of two or three feet, very compactly interlaced and circular in form. In winter they dried up and broke off at the root to be driven by the wind and distribute their seeds over the countryside.

From May to August, the waters of the Caledon were so cold that the fish all disappeared to hibernate, as we believed, and fishing came to an end. Snakes, too, disappeared. Water-fowl, snipe, partridges, and quails, hares, and the smaller kinds of antelope were as plentiful as in summer, but Eric and I had not yet reached the stage where we could hunt with a shotgun, and so we had to find other means of satisfying our tiger instincts.

22

It was about midwinter when for the first time we made the acquaintance of the Basuto herdboys from what was to us the land of mystery beyond the border; for during the winter the river fell to its lowest level, and it was then possible, even for us youngsters, to wade through the stream at a point where the bed was sandy and broad and shallow. We did not, however, attempt to cross till much later, for we had no means of knowing what reception might await us on the other side. As it was, the sight of the girls attending an initiation school, bedaubed and wearing fantastic head-dresses, and singing their weird initiation songs as they came armed with forked sticks down the opposite bank in single file, was enough to send us scampering back up the bank even before they had reached the water.

These smelly Amazons, as they seemed to us small boys, nearly terrified us out of our wits when we first saw them. Our initial fear was greatly increased by Jafta's horrifying and unprintable descriptions of what they did with their forked sticks to any male who was unfortunate enough to fall into their clutches. We never questioned the truth of these stories, but they must in part at least have been aimed at Lehaoa, who was a Basuto, because whenever Jafta mentioned the subject he cleared off. It is customary for Basuto boys to keep out of the way of girl initiates, and Lehaoa may only have been acting with proper decorum.

All through the spring and summer the Basuto herdboys, most of whom were about our age, had been watching us and our activities with as keen an interest as we felt in watching them. I have no doubt that they were as much afraid of the thing we carried that 'spat smoke and roared' as we were of their painted girls, their dogs, and their kieries or knobbed sticks. But gradually, as summer waned, a sort of long-distance communication, understanding, or what you will, had grown up between us.

Now that the river was so low, the distance between us was only fifty to seventy yards, and our keen eyes and keener curiosity had enabled us to single out individuals and dogs, and we would immediately notice the presence of a stranger. Neither side understood the other's language, yet we carried on conversations across the stream as if we understood every word of what was said, and when this game palled we resorted to various stunts in our efforts to impress each other. We would, for instance, make a mark, run up, and execute a long jump on the sand, after which we would step off the distance we had covered very deliberately and slowly, taking care that our strides should not be over-long. The other side did the same.

At other times we would go into the river where there was a quiet backwater, and in spite of the cold close our noses with thumb and forefinger, and, at a signal from a referee on one side or the other, sink below the surface to see who could remain under water the longest. Eric and I chose a spot where rushes and weeds overhung the water, and the moment we had submerged we made for cover, and then rose behind the screen, from where we watched our opponents until well after they had reappeared puffing and blowing, and slipped back to our original spot to break water. Naturally, we always won.

A little later we made a pretence of crossing to the opposite side, and soon our friends across the way tumbled to the new idea and made sorties from their side. By midwinter the water at its deepest only came up to our hips and we could easily have met in midstream; but, even after months of shouting, showing off, and miming, it was difficult to shake off our mistrust.

The day came, however, when Eric and I, accompanied by Lehaoa, at last stood facing half a dozen young Basuto herdboys six feet away in the middle of the river, each studying the other with intense and slightly anxious interest. This meeting had been initiated by Lehaoa, who had seen to it that neither side carried arms, and who now acted as interpreter.

Thereafter, full diplomatic relations were set up in an astonishingly short time, and Eric and I, each on the back of a strong herdboy, were crossing towards the Basutoland side, there to be initiated into new and strange methods of hunting.

After a time we even lost some of our fear of the 'school' girls, though the first time we saw them at close quarters was when they crossed the river to our side, and came up to within about a hundred yards of our house where we all congregated to see them in what seemed comparative safety. And it was quite obvious then that the herdboys kept discreetly out of their way.

Before we had established friendly relations with the herdboys, we had often seen them in close groups combing patches of thick grass along the banks, but we could never make out what they were up to. So now one day we shouted to them from our side to come and help us through the river.

Thebo and Quena, our two 'riding-horses', as we used to call them, came and carried us over to join the gang. They were all armed with small bows and arrows that looked rather like toys, and with kieries, and we found they were hunting striped mice. They were very fond of eating them, preferring them even to quails and partridges. These little creatures had long straight runs, up to fifty yards in length, through the patches of matted grass, and these enabled them to go far afield under cover to forage for food; then when danger threatened they ran back along the runs to their holes. Their burrows were so deep that it was impossible to dig them out, and as they were very fast and extremely timid, it was very difficult to catch them. The Basuto lads, however, had evolved a method of driving and waylaying them.

On this first day we began as mere spectators, but before long we were as enthusiastic as the herdboys themselves, so Eric joined the drivers, while I followed Thebo and two others by a roundabout way to the place where we intended waiting for the quarry. The hunters took up their positions on one side of an open patch through which a run passed, so that they could shoot at any mouse emerging on the opposite side of it, and I squatted immediately behind Thebo so that I could look over his shoulder. I was warned by signs and grimaces that I was to remain as still as a statue.

When the drive started Thebo sat with arrow fixed and bow at the ready. The drivers started about sixty yards away, and advanced slowly and as noiselessly as possible to prevent the mice from stampeding, and to give the marksmen a better chance of shooting them. Before long, we heard a slight rustling not much louder than termites might make, coming towards us. Presently, a mouse emerged into the open patch, but it must have spotted some movement, for like a flash it disappeared into the run again.

Thebo looked over his shoulder with a grimace of disgust, and resumed his vigil. Then well inside the run I saw a movement, though it was too dark to see anything clearly. The hunter waited. Then two mice appeared, one behind the other, the foremost suspiciously testing the air with its flexible and sensitive snout. At once a tiny arrow was released, and a long squeal told that it had found its mark.

In the end the hunters killed a score of mice, and then we moved into the shelter of a donga, where a fire was lit by means of fire-sticks, and soon an appetizing smell and the sizzling sound of frying mice filled the air.

Eric and I could not face eating mice or rats, thanks to our squeamishness, so we held back, hungry though we were. But Lehaoa and the other boys fell to with every sign of enjoyment. Fortunately, one of the boys, seeing us left out of the feast, ran to look at the traps near one of the threshing-floors, and returned with three quails, all for us. And how we enjoyed that meal of grilled quail, sitting for the first time round a maize-cob fire with our friends the herdboys!

These Basuto lads taught us how to set falling-stone traps, and made us presents of bows and arrows, so that in time we became almost as expert as they themselves; and we in turn initiated them into some of our ways of hunting, and more especially Hero's, that fairly astonished them.

One day eight of them crossed the river to join us in a quail hunt. We were too much excited at the prospect of the hunt to take much notice of the fact that they were accompanied by a large, fierce-looking reddish dog, who bore many battle-scars on his ears, face, and neck. But the moment he stepped onto dry land Hero closed with him, without so much as a preliminary snarl.

The Basutos were more concerned than we were, fearing that their colossus would dispose of Hero with one bite, so great was the disparity in their sizes. But in spite of our own fears we knew our Hero. His method of attacking his enemies was to grip them by the feet, a thing that no dog can stand, and it was not long before the great red creature turned tail and fled wading, swimming, and leaping over the river with Hero in hot pursuit. To the herdboys this seemed a real calamity, as their dog was an adept at flushing quails, which they then brought down with their throwing-sticks, or kieries. But we tried to console them by assuring them that Hero also was expert at the art.

We soon reached the corn-lands, where there were more quails than over the border. As we had not yet learnt the art of throwing kieries, we fell in behind the line of hunters, each of whom was walking at the ready.

Adult Basutos can direct their kieries with amazing accuracy, and I have seen them bring down at least one of every three quails that rose in front of them; but these lads were not nearly up to that standard yet, and as soon as Eric and I realized that several of the hawks called Pallid Harriers were circling above us, we advised them to cease their kierie-throwing and see how we dealt with quails.

These hawks had by now made a habit of following us, and we had come to know them so well that we had even given a name to one, a bird of lighter colour than the rest, whom we called Valie, or the Grey One. As a matter of fact, they followed us only when Hero was with us, for they had evidently come to know that it was he who flushed the quails, partridges, and snipe from their thick cover.

Quails when flushed generally fly to a distance of 100 to 200 yards before they suddenly drop into cover and stay quite still where they land. The cover in this case was rather long, matted grass. The moment a bird took to flight, one of the hawks would swoop down and follow it at breath-taking speed, often pouncing on it in full flight. But more often the quail would drop back to cover at the psychological moment and evade its pursuer. We watched closely, and as soon as a hawk had struck and missed, we raced to the place where the bird had disappeared, then stood still, so as not to disturb the scent, and, pointing to where we judged it to be hiding, said, '*Soek hom, Hero!* (Look for him, Hero!)' Having been frightened by the hawk, the quail would not move from its hiding-place, and so left no trail for the dog to follow. But Hero knew what he had to do. He first circled the spot then suddenly sprang, and pinned down the quarry with his forepaws.

The herdboys were astonished by this performance. They had never seen anything like it before and they burst into uproarious and delighted laughter. We accounted for at least a dozen quails and one partridge that day, and the hawks had soon each caught a bird and gone off to digest it at leisure.

The upshot of this day's hunting was that one sub-chief was so impressed when he heard of Hero's exploits that he offered a fat ox in exchange for the dog. Needless to say, all the cattle in Basutoland would not have tempted us to part with Hero.

Hunting the spur-wing

FROM MONDAY till Friday Eric and I had been kept so busy at school in the mornings, and in the lands helping to carry corn-sheaves to the threshing-floor in the afternoons, that hunting of any sort was out of the question. In fact our only relaxation during that week was to run down to the river for a short swim when the day's work had been completed. By the time Friday evening arrived, we were impatient, but very happy, for we had been promised that on Saturday we could have a full day to do with as we pleased. Hero had as usual read all the signs: the handling and cleaning of the old shotgun, the smell of the gunpowder, the making of shot with lead melted down and cut into strips and then into tiny squares before being finally rolled into little balls—he knew the meaning of all these. He kept wagging his tail, and was as restless as a bear in a cage.

Even before the sun rose from behind the Malutis, our sand-wiches of wholemeal bread and butter had been safely packed into a leather bag, and with that and our gun and ammunition we were

29

ready to set off. Bread and butter had become almost a luxury, for by now we had had so much experience in getting our food from the land that we could, according to the season of the year, find green mealies in our own or the Basutos' lands, murap-parappa berries, water-melons, *sewetes* (a kind of root), and bramble berries. Our allies the hawks and Hero could always be depended on to provide us with snipe, quails, or partridges, and all this could be washed down with water as crystal-clear as ever ran to the sea, from fountains along the rantjies and in the river-banks. It was indeed a life so full, free, and charming that we led, that neither riches nor the so-called blessings of modern civilization could have bettered or equalled it.

On this particular morning we had descended the rantjie, and Hero was about 200 yards ahead of us, when he started barking. There was no sign of a cobra hooded and swaying, but the dog was obviously very cautious, for he circled the spot widely with tail held straight and head low; and every now and then he would close in and then jump back swiftly as if he were avoiding a lunge or strike. When we reached the spot, we saw for the first time a really large puff-adder. As we did not want to expend a charge of our precious ammunition, I caught hold of Hero and yelled to Eric to look for stones with which to pelt the snake. There were none in the sandy soil where we were, so he had to run to the rantjie.

Finding itself unmolested for the moment, the snake made off towards some spring-hare holes; but this so excited Hero that he broke away and immediately brought it to bay again. There is a general belief that a puff-adder can only strike back-wards, but this one struck at Hero sideways, backwards, and forwards with equal ease, while the dog kept just out of range. All the time I suffered agonies of suspense as I tried to get hold of him again, for he was now so excited and enraged that he appeared not to hear my yells and pleadings, and avoided all my efforts to catch him.

It seemed an eternity while I waited for Eric's return, and I feared so much for the dog's safety that I decided to shoot the snake, only to realize that Eric was carrying the nipple-caps. The moment he arrived with the stones, I grabbed one, hurled it with all my might, and luckily hit the snake somewhere in the middle, disabling it, and between us we soon killed it. We left it where it lay, descended the bank, had a good drink, and then resumed our expedition.

Eric was not yet allowed to shoot, and I had shot nothing bigger than ducks, partridges, hares, and rock-pigeons. Our great ambition was to kill a spur-wing, one of the finest, largest and best-eating of African game-birds. But spur-wings are wary creatures, and as this was grass country and extremely flat beyond the rantjies, there were few opportunities of stalking them. We were also as yet unable to kill birds on the wing because of the weight of our weapon and our lack of experience. We were not even allowed to try because of the scarcity of ammunition. The difficulty of obtaining ammunition led to our competing with one another to kill the largest number of birds with a single shot, and I am not sure whether Stefans's twenty-five rock-pigeons, brought down as they rose from the stubble in the corn-lands, does not still stand as a record.

As we were skirting the vlei that morning, a large spur-wing rose from the grass at its edge. The bird was so heavy that it found difficulty in gaining altitude, and we watched greedily as it sailed off to some small pools in the open flats, where it settled. From the higher ground where we stood we could see numerous smaller water-fowl of various kinds in the open patches of water in the middle of the grassy vlei, and their piping and cackling never ceased. But for the moment all our interest was centred on the spur-wing, and although he was about 600 yards away his black coat and white breast were very conspicuous.

There was a fair-sized ant-heap close to us and we climbed onto it to spy out the land before deciding what to do next. We were not at all keen to go down into the vlei because of the leeches and the clinging water-weeds, dangerous when

31

one was out of one's depth; but our eyes turned hungrily towards the spur-wing, which at that moment we would rather have possessed than anything else in the world. Even at that distance we could plainly see the huge bird covering its head with its wings at almost regular intervals to preen itself, and suddenly this very natural action on its part gave me an inspiration. It was really the result of watching our cat when she hunted the tiny birds called tinktinkies, that came about our farmhouse to collect feathers to line their nests. Her method was to move forward while the bird's head was down and to freeze when it looked up. I did not see why I shouldn't try to emulate the cat.

Eric, who was a keen tinktinkie-hunter, immediately saw what I had in mind, and we soon settled on a plan of action. Eric was to sit in full view on the ant-heap, and Hero was to stay with him, while I had to stalk the bird like the cat, across the veld where there was practically no cover.

After going out of sight down the near-by river-bank, I made my way rapidly downstream till I arrived as nearly opposite to the quarry as possible, and only about 300 yards from it. To approach to within effective shooting range it was necessary to get to within thirty or forty yards.

The bird was sitting on the edge of a pool, and although there were some stunted bushes almost directly in a line between us, they were completely inadequate cover from such a keen-eyed bird, even if I were to crawl on hands and knees. So I decided to stalk it by squirming along flat on my stomach whenever it preened itself, making use at the same time of every scrap of cover that might offer.

I had gone only a few yards when I found that my greatest handicap was the gun. I could not drag it for fear of getting sand into the nipple and muzzle, so I had to lift and push it ahead of me. And when I had gone about a hundred yards I felt so tired that I thought of giving up. Three yards ahead, however, I saw a fair-sized melkbos, that offered cover and a little shade, and

I decided to reach that before making a final decision. There, gasping for breath, I first rested, and then one look at the coveted prize that was now so plainly visible was enough: I must go on.

I knew that Eric, who could see me from where he was, would remain at his post for half a day if necessary, and not to disappoint him was itself a great incentive.

The nearer I approached, the easier it became to anticipate that fraction of a second when the bird would lift its head, and the greater care I had to take to avoid detection. Once the spur-wing stopped preening sooner than I had anticipated, and I was caught with elbows crooked and chest well above the ground, and there was nothing for it but to wait in that exhausting position till the bird should drop its head again. It seemed an eternity before I could sink down to rest.

Very few creatures can distinguish a human form while it is perfectly stationary; but many are so sharp-sighted that the winking of an eye, the movement of a finger, or the slight stir of a shirt-collar in the wind will betray one's presence to them, and I knew that the spur-wing was one of them.

The movements of the bird now became more uncertain, almost as if it had had some instinctive warning of danger, and I remained glued to the ground for a long time before I ventured to proceed again. Slowly I crawled nearer, till at last I arrived at a small bush about forty yards from the quarry. My heart was beating so violently from exhaustion and excitement that it would have been impossible to fire immediately.

Eventually I managed to fit a cap while the bird was preening; but although I was aiming from a prone position I shook like a leaf from nervousness and fatigue. I took a second breath, concentrated with all my might, and then pulled the trigger. Some feathers shot up and then came spiralling down; but the beautiful creature spread its wings and sailed away, leaving me dumbfounded and utterly cast down. Dazed with disappointment, I watched the retreating bird. But as I looked, I saw more feathers come spiralling down, and then he made straight for the vlei losing altitude fast. Suddenly his wings folded and he came hurtling down, but the rise between prevented me from seeing where he had landed.

Just then I heard Eric shouting and saw him gesticulating wildly and pointing towards the vlei, and I knew that he was keeping his eye on the place where the spur-wing had dropped. A few minutes later I stood on the ant-heap beside him, and could plainly see the dead bird as it lay in a clear patch in the middle of the vlei about 150 yards away.

Desire now banished my fear and made me quite reckless. Only a short hour earlier I should not have dreamed of going into the vlei to where the bird was now floating, for fear of pot-holes, blood-suckers, and entangling water-weeds; and here I was casting shirt and trousers aside!

As I waded in, the water gradually got deeper, and when I had covered about half the distance, it already came up to my waist. Owing to the covering of weeds, the sun could never penetrate the water, and the deeper I went the colder it became, till at last I gasped for breath as it crept up to my chest, and the fear of becoming entangled in the weeds caused me to shiver as much as the cold itself did. At length the bird was only ten yards away, but the water was getting deeper, and swimming was out of the question, so I had to advance very slowly inch by inch.

Once the water suddenly came up to my mouth as I trod into a depression, and I had to try in various directions for a footing. At long last, however, I managed to get hold of the spur-wing, and turned to retrace my steps. But I had gone only a few yards when the water suddenly got deeper, and I had to back hurriedly. I thought I was returning the same way I had come, and I looked to see where Eric was; but to my horror he was nowhere to be seen, as the long grass near the edges of the vlei shut out the view. I tried two different directions, but on each occasion found myself going out of my depth, and had hurriedly to flounder back to my former position. I now realized that I had completely lost my direction. 'If only I could see Eric,' I thought. But I was afraid to shout for him lest he should come to my assistance and also get into difficulties.

I was so cold, miserable, and panic-stricken, that I was on the point of abandoning the spur-wing when suddenly, ten yards away, Hero appeared swimming strongly towards me. He had followed on my spoor, which the floating leaves made possible, and he was coming from a direction exactly opposite to where in my confused state I had thought he and Eric were.

With my courage once more restored I grabbed the bird and set out again. Then, as I jumped up to snatch breath, for the first time I felt the entangling weeds, and I almost despaired. I unconsciously let go of the bird; but Hero, as if it were the most natural thing in the world, retrieved it, and half-dragged, half-pushed, it up to me. I fought free of the weeds, and not long after, while still laboriously wading waist-deep, I was joined by Eric.

My whole body was covered with leeches, and we removed them while I stood shivering in the hot sun that was beating down on us.

It was now only about half past nine, but we were so keen to display our prize that we decided to go home at once. Our recital of the morning's doings was freely punctuated by exclamations of admiration from Lehaoa and Jafta; but Father thought the moment opportune to say, 'I hope you understand now why I have warned you of the dangers of water-weeds'.

We did. But the day was young, and we were not going to be robbed of a moment of it; and so, having had a mug of coffee each, we were off to the vleis once more, to return at sunset tired out but supremely happy, having shot a number of yellow-billed ducks, having collected a mixed bag of quails and snipe accounted for by Hero and the hawks, and having eaten our fill of the many good things that only those who lived as we did could have found and enjoyed.

Graatjie the Meerkat

THE STOKSTERT or graatjie meerkat, not unlike a mongoose, weighs only about two and a half pounds when fully grown. He is a reddish-brown little creature with a sharply pointed muzzle and a straight, thin tail from which he takes his popular name of stokstert, or stick-tailed, meerkat. He is a very likable creature, and is easily tamed, partly because he eats everything, with his unusually strong jaws and teeth, but chiefly because of his docile temper. Once he has been tamed, he will never bite a human being unless he has been illtreated, and then like a monkey, a baboon, or an elephant, he neither forgets nor forgives.

One day a friend and I were walking across the veld when we met a family of graatjies on the move. My friend was a good sprinter, and decided that he wanted to catch a youngster, only about a third grown, that we saw struggling in the rear. He managed to overhaul the little creature and caught hold of it. Like a flash, however, it fastened on to the point of his thumb, piercing nail and flesh with its sharp teeth. The bite was so painful that he instinctively flung it from him, and it landed in a small bush yards away; but it promptly picked itself out and dashed off on the spoor of its friends.

Graatjies are gregarious, and one often comes across a family of twenty or more. They sometimes share the burrows of other species of meerkats, when there is plenty of room, but if there is a housing shortage they will expel the rightful owners without any qualms of conscience. In fact, I often wonder how much burrowing they do themselves.

They remain in one spot as long as there is sufficient to eat, and when they have moved on, there is seldom an insect, worm, lizard, or snake left in the vicinity. They are inveterate snake-killers.

One day a very young graatjie was presented to Eric by a pedlar, and for years we kept him as a pet. Right from the start 'Graatjie', as we called him, made it abundantly clear that he called no one his master, and he asserted his superiority over all living beings in the farmhouse, whether human or animal. Everything he did was done in a slow, cool, and methodical way. He loved to be handled by members of the family, curling up and snuggling close as he 'curk-curked' his satisfaction; but when he was making for any objective he was not to be turned from it by restraining hands, and he would with patient persistence disengage himself over and over, never losing his temper unless he was roughly handled.

One day, he found Jafta's pipe fully charged lying on the stoep, and after a minute inspection started scratching the tobacco from the container. He did not stop till every scrap was removed and he then tried to force his tiny paw into the aperture of the stem, thinking, no doubt, 'This is just the place to find a worm'.

Another day, as I opened a door leading into the back yard, he was at my feet making his curking noise. I stooped to pick him up for a chat, but he instantly made a bee-line for a tree eleven yards from where I stood, stopped suddenly, began to dig straight down, and unearthed a large fat brown worm, which he ate with the utmost relish. I have often wondered how he knew the worm was there. A learned naturalist has suggested that he scented it; but the worm was not only eleven yards away but several inches beneath the soil.

We started an ash-heap in the back yard, intending to use it as fertilizer. Often, live coals that got buried beneath the pile sent up thin columns of smoke through the ashes. One cold winter's morning, I saw Graatjie moving about the heap and I watched him to see what he was after. He approached one of the smoke spirals and scratched all around it till the glowing ember was exposed. Then he came up close to it and sat straight up with his sparsely covered belly almost touching it. I realized then that he was trying to warm himself, and that he looked upon the ember as his heater. I do not know how he had got the idea, but after this he made frequent use of his 'heaters' on cold days.

He was on good terms with an angora kid that had lost its mother, and was being bottle-fed. All went well until the kid started butting playfully, a form of amusement that must have annoyed Graatjie greatly, because one day we saw the kid careering around, bleating agonizedly, with Graatjie hanging on to its soft loin skin. Thereafter the kid avoided the meerkat like the devil himself, while the meerkat was content to ignore his former playmate completely.

Aunt Sarie disliked pets; even Hero sensed this, and would growl on the rare occasions when he saw her. The first time she saw Graatjie, he was about six months old. She instantly took a strong dislike to him, and promptly earned Eric's hearty detestation by telling him to 'take the stinking thing away'. He did so, but Graatjie was soon back again, sidling up to her swinging foot with his usual friendly confidence in people. What she did to him we never knew—she told us later that she had merely swept him aside several times with her shoe —but she so enraged the usually good-natured animal that he fastened his sharp teeth in the toe of her shoe, and it took brute force to prize loose his hold. Luckily, she was not hurt, but her feelings were outraged, and it was about six months before

Aunt Sarie turned up again. One day, when next she was on a visit to us, Mother was in bed, and I was in the back yard helping Father, when we heard a high-pitched yell coming from the front of the house. We ran round to find Aunt Sarie sprawling in the dust with Graatjie sticking like a tick to her heel. His teeth had penetrated so deeply that when we managed to get him off the blood poured out. The little scamp had not forgotten his enemy. Aunt Sarie was so incensed and my parents were so upset that there was talk of doing away with our pet. Eventually a compromise was reached, and it was agreed that Graatjie would be kept under lock and key whenever the old lady visited us; but by this time Eric had disappeared into the rantjies, meerkat and all, only to return at dusk.

Winter was well on the way when we first got Graatjie, and although a snug little nest was prepared for him he spent the first night and, for that matter, most subsequent winter nights, under Eric's blankets.

We always had to be on the look-out for strange dogs that might attack the meerkat; and it was only owing to our constant watchfulness that he survived to a good old age.

Then, early one morning, a large mongrel came nosing around the house, and as usual Hero attacked the moment he saw the intruder. Eric was the first to hear the commotion and he ran out to investigate. The mongrel had fastened on to Hero's loose neck-skin while the latter was trying to grab a forepaw. Graatjie had been dodging around looking for an opening, and Eric was just in time to see him sink his sharp teeth into one of the mongrel's hind feet. At this the mongrel swung round, seized the meerkat, and slung him several yards away. This gave Hero his opportunity, and he grabbed and held on to a paw, and soon ended the fight. But the victory was small consolation to us, for Graatjie, although he tried, was unable to pick himself up again. He was mortally wounded and died in Eric's hands, game to the last.

My first yellow-fish

I HAD my first sight of a large yellow-fish only a few days after we arrived at Alpha. The stream at that time was clear, as the summer rains had not yet started.

For two or three days Eric and I sat for long spells on the bank of the river watching the fish rise and splash, a new and fascinating pastime. We did not, however, see the fish themselves, as the days were either cloudy or windy, and if one is to be able to see fish, even in clear water, there must be little or no wind and a cloudless sky. The third or fourth day broke fine and clear, and hardly a ripple disturbed the deeper stretches of water—ideal conditions for seeing fish swimming near the surface.

We had been on the bank for only a few minutes, when suddenly, just where the stream entered the pool, we both saw a golden flash, but no definite shape. Not long after, however, we made out two forms gradually rising towards the top. At first they were in the shade cast by the bank, but as they passed into sunshine they suddenly assumed a colour so richly golden that we gasped in admiration. We had never before seen fish weighing more than two or three pounds, for the spruit on the farm where we had been born had only *kalwerkop* (literally, 'calf's head') and mudfish, and the size of the yellow-fish astonished us.

For a long time these two cruised around, and we could not take our fascinated eyes off them. Then Hero, who had followed on our spoor, came up to us in his boisterous way, and the fish instantly disappeared, although we were about forty yards away from them.

After this we gave Father no rest until he had fixed up a hook and line for us. The line was about twenty-five yards long, and the hook strong enough to hold any fresh-water fish. He also gave us an iron peg to push deep into the sand, and then baited the hook with a frog, and soon we were able to cast our bait where the stream entered the pool. We waited eagerly for a bite, but as our movements so near the water's edge could plainly be seen by the fish, nothing happened; so after a time we got bored and went home, leaving our tackle to take care of itself.

About half an hour later I went back to the river alone. As I came over the bank above the pool I heard a loud splash, and saw a disturbance in the water where the bait had been cast. On coming closer, I found that the peg had been pulled forward so much as to leave a cut in the wet sand, and most of the line itself had been pulled under the sand.

I released the peg, and at that moment a violent jerk caused me to lose my balance, and I came down full length, still holding on to the peg. In getting up, I put one foot into a dry thorn-bush that had got covered by the drifting sand, and the excruciating pain made me let go my hold of the peg. I immediately saw it racing swiftly towards the water's edge and made a last desperate effort to catch up with it; but alas, I was too late, and peg and line disappeared into the dark green water. I think only the pain in my foot prevented me from shedding tears.

Eric and I were now determined to get even with the yellow-fish, and next day we got another hand-line, and cast it at the same spot. Then we retired up the bank to watch. In due course we saw, not a couple, but dozens of fishes cruising around, some almost on the surface, and we were in high hopes that we would get a bite almost immediately, but for half an hour nothing happened.

Then, just as Eric stood up to stretch himself, the line suddenly came to life. A golden form shot up into the sunshine and then hit the water about four feet from where it had emerged. We jumped down the bank and I hung on to the peg, while Eric seized the line. Neither of us had ever seen a rod or reel, and our idea of landing a fish was to haul it in as quickly as possible. But the fish made us revise our ideas by putting up a desperate struggle. If our line had not had a breaking strain of about twenty pounds, and our hook been equally strong, something must have parted.

We now remembered Father's injunction to 'stand firm, and let the fish do the pulling', and this we proceeded to put into practice. Eric's hands were cut so badly that on several occasions he let go, and each time I was hard put to it to keep a firm purchase with my toes in the soft sand. Gradually, however, the fish began to tire.

I handed the peg to Eric, and went towards the water, allowing the line to slip slowly through my hands. After our fight we knew we might expect to see a strong fish, but what we saw at the water's edge was beyond our hopes, and I trembled for fear we might lose it. It turned on its side and then onto its back, a sign that it had reached the end of its tether.

I shouted to Eric to come and help me, and in less time than it takes to tell we were dragging our prize away from the water, so excited that we hardly knew what we were doing. Its mouth was so large that I could put my two clenched fists into it, and it weighed twenty-two and a half pounds But it was not so much its size that impressed us as its beautiful proportions and vivid golden colour. Since then I have landed large yellow-fish too numerous to mention; but the sight of that glorious creature was what first gave me 'fishing fever'.

It was just such a golden beauty that on another occasion nearly caused our death in a very inglorious fashion. We had caught a yellow-fish full of roe, and as my parents were out for the day, we decided to have its roe for supper, we children,

Lehaoa, and Jafta. Shortly after we had eaten it we were all as sick as could be, and we spent a long night of retching before we slowly recovered next day. We learned later that at certain seasons the roe of the yellow-fish becomes poisonous. After that experience, however, at no season would any of us touch it again.

The Caledon at that time offered excellent opportunities of studying these fishes. In the summer months, before the river came down in flood, the waters were so clear that on a sunny day one could see schools of all ages swimming around in the deeper places. I remember a perpendicular wall where, peering down, one could see to the sandy bottom. Here scores of yellow-fishes congregated, and we often played out our lines quietly till the bait touched the heads of some of the fish; but for some reason they took no notice at all of any kind of bait, and merely moved away a foot or two, after which they invariably resumed their interrupted siesta. Yet only about 200 yards from this spot, in deeper water, one seldom waited long for a bite.

The changes that have come over the veld during the last fifty or sixty years have destroyed the conditions that favour yellow-fish. The thickly matted grass and scrub that have now disappeared, caught up every drop of rain and ensured the strong running streams vital to them. In addition, the hardier carp that has so firmly established itself in all but a few streams and dams in the country, is ousting this beautiful and timid fish, which may well be called the queen of the rivers.

As well as being beautiful and dignified, it is a clean and fastidious creature, and will touch no meat-bait that is not absolutely fresh. It is, indeed, difficult to understand how such aristocrats can live side by side with the ugly, greedy barbel or the unpalatable mudfish. Actually, while these can thrive in dams and standing pools, the yellow-fish degenerates or disappears when it is deprived of fresh, strongly running water.

Part Two

A DIVERSITY OF CREATURES

More yellow-fish

NOBODY TAUGHT ME as much about the art of catching yellow-fish as Louis Fleck did. Even when he was well over 70, this was not merely his only sport, but his obsession. I have never seen his equal in handling a hooked fish, and he could land any fish with machine-thread of a breaking strain of only about six pounds. He always selected his fishing spots very carefully, and he never used a landing-net or gaff. He first of all made sure that he could reach down from the bank to the water, and that no obstructions such as branches or tree-stumps should limit the space he needed to play his quarry.

In standing water he would also test the bottom by dragging a sinker over it, and when he was satisfied that all was well he would cast his lines, light his pipe, and settle behind a screen of his own making if there was no natural cover, to commence his vigil. Ensconced there, he would be as immovable as a cat for at least half an hour, when he would rebait his hooks. He used a double hook made of two small hooks tied back to back.

I used to marvel at the way he landed heavy catches with his inferior reels, weak lines, and stiff rods, and I watched his methods very carefully. Every few seconds he would give the line a tug, but so circumspectly that it was never in danger of parting. 'These tugs', he explained, 'serve as a series of shocks which sap the courage and strength of the fish.' And the reason he gave me for using stiff rods was that when the fish was close in he could push it out and away from roots and other obstructions close to the bank. 'Also,' he added, 'the real art, and fun, of landing a big fish is to play it from the reel, and not to depend on the elasticity of the rod or the strength of the line.'

He took careful note of all the conditions—the weather, the direction of the wind, the temperature of the water, whether it was standing or running—and the sort of bait that was right for the time of the year. On arriving at a new fishing-spot he would study the surrounding countryside, note the kind of soil and vegetation, and judge from that whether the bottom of the pool would probably consist of sand, mud, gravel, hard pot-clay, or stone.

He scorned the idea of weighing a fish. 'You can weigh a fish and afterwards add fifty per cent of its weight to your story, and who will be the wiser? But if you keep their jaw bones and teeth to show, who can then doubt your word?' Yellow-fish have long and sharp teeth at the back of their jaws, and Louis had collected some of enormous size.

He would only tell his fishing experiences to those he knew really well. 'Most people', he would say, in his soft-spoken way, 'just think that they are listening to fishing yarns.'

He fought on the side of the republics throughout the Anglo-Boer War, but often said he hoped he had never been the cause of the loss of a human life. 'But', he added, 'I provided our men with fish whenever the opportunity offered, particularly during the closing stages when we were on the verge of starvation, and I remember my last day's fishing on commando as clearly as if it happened yesterday.'

I had at last got him talking as we sat on a river-bank. Just then he had a bite, struck, and missed, baited his lines again, lit his pipe, and once more settled behind our screen of branches, and to my relief and delight he continued as if there had been no interruption.

'One day our Commandant was ill. He could not eat kaboemielies and the lean meat that was all we had, and so I decided to try and catch fish for him. He was a man I had a great liking for.

'I had already tried for yellow-fish that morning but had no luck, for which I blamed the thick line and large hook I was using.

'It was very dry, and the Vaal River was running low, and I could get neither grasshoppers, crabs, nor frogs for bait, but eventually, after a good deal of hunting around, I found about a dozen earthworms beneath driftwood close to the water.

'The sun was low when at last I sat waiting on the side of a quiet backwater, without much hope of a bite. We were practically surrounded by the enemy and I knew we were due to try and give them the slip when darkness came; and here I was fishing a mile away from the laager.

'One by one my precious earthworms were nibbled off by small fishes, and when I was making what must be my last cast, only half the hook was covered.

'Suddenly my line started moving and I knew at once that there was a large fish at the other end. I waited till I felt the pull and then struck, and I felt that I had hooked something very heavy. Soon I was engaged in a tug-of-war such as I had never experienced before with a fish. I realized that it could not be a yellow, and immediately after, some bubbles rose to the surface and confirmed my suspicions that it was a barbel.

'I gradually worked him round into a narrow creek, but he skulked under the bank, and by this time my hands were badly cut by the line.

'Then I looked about and saw a youth about to herd the horses back towards the laager, so I called him to come and give me a hand. I gave him the line, took off my clothes, and went into the water, which came up to my chin. Gingerly feeling my way down the line with my toes I presently touched a head so large that I could hardly believe it belonged to a barbel. The touch, however, had the desired effect of making him move, and the youth on the bank shouted for me to come and help him.

'By now the fish was tiring and before long I was able to insert my hand into its gills and drag it on to the bank; but not before it had splashed me with mud from head to foot.'

'How large was it,' I asked.

'Well, we had no means of weighing it,' answered Louis. 'Some of our men thought it was in the neighbourhood of 120 pounds; and mark you, he took that bit of earthworm when his stomach already contained two large mudfish and a coot!'

Looking thoughtful and knocking out his pipe, Louis added, 'If that barbel had only had the sense, he could have drowned any man that swam in deep water.

'We cut the meat into strips and made biltong of it, and for days afterwards the Commandant had all the fish he wanted.'

A thing that has greatly puzzled me is what happens to old yellow-fish. When a fish dies, sooner or later it floats to the surface, unless something makes a meal of it; but in all my experience I have seen only one large yellow-fish on the surface that had apparently died from natural causes. Yet it is common to see small dead yellow-fish, mudfish, and kalwerkops drifting on the water or being eaten by crabs on the banks.

That crabs dispose of the big ones before they rise to the surface can be ruled out, for wherever there are yellow-fish barbel are also to be found in large numbers, and the barbel is the crab's most deadly enemy. No crab will venture out into deep water where there are barbel.

Another question to which I have found no satisfactory answer is that of the yellow-fish's diet. In the Kaffir River dam near Bloemfontein, in which, luckily, there are no carp, the largest yellow-fish reach a weight of possibly eighteen to twenty pounds. This is not large when compared to the giants of the Orange, Vaal, and a few of the smaller rivers, but nowhere else in Africa can such fat or perfect specimens be found. Yet there is exceedingly little vegetation in the dam, which is used for purposes of irrigation. Then, too, it is only on the rare occasions when the dam is full that there is any likelihood of grasshoppers and other insects falling into the water, and crabs are kept down to the barest minimum by the voracious barbels. Nor are these yellow-fish cannibals; in fact in this dam they will not touch small fishes.

The only explanation seems to be that they live on the microscopic vegetable organisms in the water, drawing them in through their mouths and sifting them through their gills. Whatever the explanation, the yellow-fish here are in superlative condition all the year round.

There is probably no sport in the world that can count amongst its devotees so many curious characters, with such a variety of professions, as can be found amongst fishermen. I remember a day when I had as my companions a Provincial Administrator and a chimney-sweep, and we were as happy as sandboys. If ever a sport can be called a true leveller, it is fishing.

There was 12-year-old Evertjie, who lived in the Kroonstad district. By the time I met him, I was old enough to be his father, and yet during the school vacations he and I were almost inseparable; and we saw much more of the Rhenoster spruit and the surrounding dams than of the inside of his parents' spacious farmhouse.

One day we were fishing at the lower end of the large Koppies dam. Whether Evertjie had had a bad night or the sun was too hot, I frequently found him dosing instead of watching his line, so I tied a large red float on to it to keep him interested. It had the desired effect, and presently the float began to bob and it was obvious that something was nibbling at the bait.

Suddenly there was a loud 'whap!', and the float was gone. Evertjie struck, but there was no resistance, and what was left of the line fell back limply. The look of astonishment on his face was ludicrous.

Then, a hundred yards away the float came to the surface in the deep water; no doubt a misguided barbel that had imagined it to be a live morsel had found out his mistake!

A little later, as we had had no bites, I climbed the koppie immediately behind us, leaving Evertjie with the rods. The water was clear, and from where I stood I could see large barbel swimming close to the surface, but not a trace of yellow-fish.

Suddenly, some distance to my right, my eye caught a movement about five yards from the side, and presently I made out two objects slowly swimming in our direction. I at once realized that they were large yellow-fish looking for food; but as they were swimming close in I knew they could not spot our bait, which was cast far out in deep water.

I ran down, told Evertjie to hide behind a near-by rock, and reeled in one of my lines till the bait was hanging straight down from the point of the rod, about two feet below the surface and about as far from the edge. Having done this, I lay down at full length behind the rod, holding on to it with one hand, and kept quite still. Lying flat on the ground, I could see very little, but after what seemed an age a ring of small wavelets moved the line. I lifted my head slightly, and for an instant saw the dorsal fin of a large fish cutting the surface. Then I could plainly see the dark golden creature circling the bait. Two or three times it swam around, and I knew that it was a matter of seconds before it would either overcome its suspicions and seize the bait or else move away. I had never been so near to a large yellow-fish without its being aware of me, and my heart was thumping with excitement.

Then, so quickly did it seize the bait that the reel screeched at the same instant that I saw it turn inwards. It was so close, and the pull was so severe, that all I could do was to give it a free run till it had ended its first mad rush. Evertjie, who had never seen a large yellow-fish before, was very excited, and while the fish was being played he kept on saying, 'If only the line won't break! Pray that the line won't break!' The line held.

A week later, Evertjie and I were fishing in the river just below the railway-bridge, where the stream was running strongly. We cast our lines in a backwater at the top end of a high bank. Above it there was a patch of mimosas, whose roots protruded where the ground had been washed away by the summer floods, while lower down, beyond the wall, the banks were clear of trees.

Presently I got a bite, but the moment I struck, the trace broke. Five minutes later, however, I had a second bite on the same line. This time I knew that I had hooked something heavy; the fish was fighting downstream and as I had only fifty yards of line on my reel I realized that soon there would be no more left to play with.

As there was an almost sheer drop into the water from the wall, with only the protruding roots between, I had either to plunge into the water, clothes, boots, and all, and swim past the wall, or crawl like a fly along it, holding on to the roots with one hand. I chose the latter course and negotiated it under the stress of the moment, as I could not have done in cold blood.

So far, I had no idea whether I was dealing with barbel, yellow-fish, or carp, but the moment I was clear of the wall the fish shot out towards midstream again, and a large yellow tail appeared for a moment on the surface. The fish now went downstream so fast, and was so strong, that for a time I could do nothing but follow in its wake. There were three small islands in midstream, and the fish kept trying to pass round the far side, and I had to give judicious tugs to prevent it. At last, just above a large pool where the river was broad and shallow, I landed the largest yellow-fish I ever caught with rod and reel. It weighed eighteen and a half pounds.

While trying to dislodge the hook from the side of its mouth I saw, to my astonishment, that the hook I had lost at the first strike was firmly embedded in almost the same spot.

The Ratel

ONE DAY in 1933, I arrived at the Wilmot's farm at Highlands, near Grahamstown.

One of the brothers, Richmond, who was my special hunting companion, received me with his usual enthusiasm; but I noticed an added excitement in his manner, and I soon learned the cause of it. Richmond was the hunter and naturalist of the family, but lately he had had to hunt jackals almost to the exclusion of all else; for the Wilmots were, and still are, some of the most successful sheep-farmers in the country, and the jackals had been playing havoc with their flocks.

To be able to cope with jackals the first requirement is to possess good hunting-dogs, for jackals are wily at avoiding traps and poisoned bait as perhaps no other animal is. Richmond, who already possessed a dog called Airedale, actually a cross between an Airedale and an Irish terrier, had just acquired another dog; and the cause of the excitement was a battle royal between the two dogs. As Richmond said, 'I had to allow them to fight it out, or they would never have settled down—and the stranger won. This had been Airedale's first defeat.'

My curiosity was aroused and we went to look at the dogs. Airedale was lean, long-legged, and much larger than I had expected. The other dog, whose name was 'Inja', was a cross between nothing I could think of and a greyhound. Pale-brown stripes rather like a zebra's covered his whole dusky-coloured body and he was even leaner and longer-legged than Airedale.

I asked Richmond where he had acquired this strange animal and he said that passing a hut on an adjoining farm at sundown, he had stopped to speak to a chief who lived there, and seen the dog with him. A jackal had started calling about half a mile away, and the chief spun round and, pointing in the direction from which the sound came, said, 'All right, we are coming,' obviously meaning the dog and himself. 'Can he kill a jackal?' asked Richmond, and by way of replying the chief dived into his hut and came back with the skins of several recently killed jackals and a lynx. That was enough for Richmond, and he at once decided that Inja must be his, no matter what his price.

Soon after my arrival, I saw Inja in a fight, and then I was not surprised that he had overcome the redoubtable Airedale. He was fighting a large half-breed bulldog, and the bulldog never had the least chance of getting a stranglehold, for Inja would rush in, grab a mouthful, and then jerk backwards like a wild dog. I even saw him jumping clean over the back of his opponent in order to attack from a new angle.

As Richmond had predicted, Airedale and Inja soon became friendly, and instead of fighting each other co-operated against whatever had to be fought.

I had come for a long holiday, and so Richmond and I set about exterminating jackals with the aid of the dogs; and we were so successful that before long there was not a sign of a jackal on their farm, and we were able to switch over to our favourite sport of hunting bushbuck.

One cloudy day we were skirting the foot of the Carlsrust Mountain, where a deep, dry donga emerged from the thick bush, when we heard the dogs barking about half a mile away. They had gone on ahead of us, and we now set out in their direction. By the time we reached the spot where we had expected to find them they were nowhere to be seen, and the barking had ceased. We stood wondering what to do, when we heard a muffled sound coming from higher up the donga, and set off in that direction. As the going became rough and boulder-strewn, we climbed down into the dry bed of the donga, which was partly sandy, and here Richmond found the spoor of the dogs, and also that of another animal which he could not identify.

We followed the spoor and soon arrived at a clearing inside a bush, where we saw the dogs fighting something, but we could not at first make out what, as the dogs were on top of it. Then as he and I got closer Richmond said quietly, 'ratel', and at once I was all agog. My one previous encounter in the Bushveld with a ratel, or honey badger, made me most eager now to see all I could of the fight with this little black-and-white devil, of which I had heard so many stories since I was a child.

In their efforts to keep down the ratel, the dogs almost covered it, but it turned and twisted like a hooked eel, and was continually freeing itself.

The two dogs, so well trained, tough, and capable, that they had won a hundred furious battles against jackals, lynxes, and baboons, and had once even killed an almost fully grown leopard, were fighting a losing battle against an opponent that was only about a fifth of their combined weights. Their tongues were lolling, and blood was oozing from numerous punctures on their bodies.

Inja was bleeding at the mouth, and we could see that he was in a bad way. His throat had been badly hurt, and soon he came over and stood to one side, utterly crestfallen.

When Richmond realized the danger to his dogs, he tried to shoot the game little battler, but dog and ratel were so inextricably mixed that there was danger of his shooting both together. Eventually, however, he managed to kill the ratel.

We had to carry the injured dog over the long distance that separated us from home, and for days his only sustenance was what little milk he could swallow. However, he eventually pulled through. As for Airedale, although he did not fare as badly as Inja, he was nevertheless crippled for the better part of a week.

Anyone who does not know the ratel may find it hard to credit such ferocity in so small an animal. Lt.-Col. Stevenson-Hamilton, the famous game warden of the Kruger National Park, in his book *Animal Life in South Africa* has this to say about the ratel:

'This animal, akin to and about the size of a true badger, is remarkable in several ways, and excites my own admiration and respect to a higher degree than any other beast which roams the African jungle . . . the fore claws are very long and powerful, and the skin is so extraordinarily tough and loose, that it is impervious alike to the teeth of the largest dog, the fangs of the most venomous snake or the stings of attacking bees.'

After giving a description of the alliance which exists between the birds called the 'honey-guides' and the ratel for the purpose of robbing insect's nests, Lt.-Col. Stevenson-Hamilton continues:

'I do not believe there exists in the world a more absolutely courageous animal than the ratel. He seems to fear nothing that runs, flies or crawls. I have known cases when after a protracted struggle with a pack of dogs, the ratel has picked himself up and jogged off leaving his assailants totally exhausted and all more or less damaged.

'On another occasion a patrolling ranger came to a spot where a lion had tackled a ratel, and had only succeeded in killing the game little beast after a severe struggle, of which the trampled bush and grass supplied a faithful record. After his victory the lion had found little relish in the meat for he had eaten only a very little of it.'

Mr David van Niekerk, an octogenarian of Roodeheuwel near Bloemfontein, told me of an encounter he and some of his friends had with a ratel when he was about 12 years old. I shall give the story as he told it:

'The ratel was caught by one foreleg in a very strong steel trap, and with a great deal of difficulty we managed to bring him to the homestead. It was a Sunday morning and we had only just got home when the bell rang for the midday service, which in those days lasted for at least one and a half hours. Our "gang", which consisted of some of my brothers and cousins, had to hurry indoors, and not knowing for the moment what to do with our ratel we suddenly got the idea of lifting one of the front wheels of the wagon, and placing it on the neck of the squirming little beast.

'By this time we had been sprayed with the ratel's strong-smelling effluvia, and made desperate but futile efforts to rid ourselves of the smell before going in to service. Even an attacking swarm of bees cannot stand the musky smell of a ratel attacking its nest, and I am sure no man, however pious, sincere, or deeply absorbed could possibly ignore it.

'It is a moot point whether any one of us afterwards remembered a word of what had been read or said; but I know this much, that the service that morning lasted no longer than half an hour, instead of the customary hour and a half.

'When we eventually lifted the wagon-wheel, the ratel seemed to be dead, but in a very few minutes he came to life again, and caught and splintered a stick that had been aimed at him.

'At last my father shot him, for by this time we did not believe he could be killed in any other way.'

As a matter of fact a ratel can be made a pet of, and when treated with kindness is particularly charming as well as quite harmless. And to see him jog-trotting along quietly, making his way through the bush, one would hardly guess how ferocious he can be when roused. Perhaps the most curious thing about him is that an animal possessing such toughness and fighting qualities should also be able to discharge an odour so obnoxious as to confound and demoralize most of its enemies.

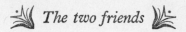 *The two friends*

MANY STORIES have been written about friendships, mythical or real, between wild animals, even between those that belong to different species. Such as I have met with have usually been between old antelope bulls that have been ousted by younger and more virile leaders. But I once came across a friendship between two small animals of different species, both of whom may have been outcasts.

On the northern boundary of my home town of Bloemfontein there are low ranges of hills where, protected by the farmers who own the land, a surprising variety of the smaller kinds of animals still roam. There are rhebok, duiker and steenbok antelope, three different kinds of hares, jackals, partridges, guinea-fowl, and various other smaller types of animals and birds. And from the direction of Quin's farm and the hills of the Van Tonders, baboons sometimes range to within three miles of the city.

I have spent a good deal of time wandering in these hills, and among them there is a kloof so quiet and remote that it might almost be on faraway Letaba, Radoo, or Tau Loomi, except for an occasional aeroplane that passes overhead, and that hardly obtrudes on one's consciousness.

On a certain rise not far from this kloof I frequently flushed a steenbok ram. At first the dainty little buck used to dash off wildly till he was lost to view over the rise. Finding by degrees, however, that I was harmless and made no approaches, he gradually lost his fear of me. I always gave a gentle 'cooee' when he jumped up, and he soon appeared to distinguish between me and an occasional herdboy or trespasser that came his way, for he stopped at my signal, looked round listening, and in due course often returned to where he had been lying even before I was out of sight. But he never stopped closer than about a hundred yards from me.

57

One day as I approached, I saw his head and large ears above a patch of short brush, and for the first time I had the opportunity of 'cooee-ing' while he was still recumbent; and to my great satisfaction he allowed me to come within a hundred yards before he trotted off slowly, stopping every now and then to look round.

As I neared the spot where he had been lying up, a *vlakhaas*, or Cape hare, flushed almost at my feet, and I could see by his red flanks and lean appearance that he was a male. It suddenly occurred to me that on a number of occasions I had seen a hare exactly like this one jump up close to where the steenbok had been resting. After that, I kept a look-out, and whenever I roused the buck, which was not, of course, always in the same spot, I never failed to find the hare close by.

Soon I had little doubt that these two were friends, and to make doubly sure I watched through my binoculars from a near-by

koppie one day just as the sun was setting and the shadows were gathering in the kloof.

At first there was nothing to be seen, and then the hare came into view, alternately nibbling and sitting up on its haunches to look round. Within a few minutes the buck daintily picked his way from the brush-covered ridge to join his friend at a green patch close to the fountain.

I watched till it was so late that I had to hurry to get over the ridge before darkness overtook me, as there was no moon; but I was now completely satisfied that the hare and the steenbok were inseparable companions. And on many occasions after that I saw the incongruous pair together.

One day, about a week after a severe storm, I missed them, and as the ground was still moist I looked for their spoor, as I had often done in the past. Now, however, I received a shock when my eyes fell on the spoor of a dog that had been running very fast. The speed at which the animal had travelled, and the size of the spoor, left no doubt in my mind that the prints were those of a greyhound, and I could tell from the state of broken grass-blades that the tracks had been made about twenty-four hours earlier.

Casting around, I found that three dogs had taken part in the chase, and soon I discovered what I hoped I would not find, the tracks of a steenbok running at its fastest.

On the moist ground the spoor was easy to follow; the terrain was part grass and part brush-covered, and almost devoid of stones. 'You little fool,' I said desperately. 'Why didn't you turn to the broken ground on the left?' I hurried on, still half-hoping, but soon came to a spot where the buck had turned sharply, and, 300 yards further on, it had been pulled down. There were all the marks, and in addition to the other tracks, the footprints of a man.

There was still an hour to sunset, and I sat down on an antheap to try to reconstruct what had happened. I remembered that a month earlier I had seen a man, accompanied by several greyhounds, wandering along the ridges about two miles to the east, and I thought it was most probable that it was these dogs that had run down the steenbok, but of course I could not be sure. However, as I had my binoculars with me, I decided to climb the koppie and look out for the hare.

The sun was about to set, and its rays were shining on to a few isolated clouds higher up, when I scanned the darkening valley, and there, coming out of the brush and hobbling along towards the green patch, was the hare. When he reached the edge of the grass, he sat up on his haunches and for a long time remained so motionless that my eyes became tired with watching the spot. When he moved again, it was no more than a foot or two, only to assume the same rocklike immobility. Not once while I looked did he feed, and I knew beyond any doubt that he was waiting for his friend. Not a breath of air stirred. The silvery rims that circled the stationary clouds had almost vanished, and a sombre peacefulness had settled on the hazy hills when I took a last look, and there in the growing dusk, still waiting and watching, sat the lonely hare.

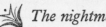

The nightmare-bird and others

LATE ONE AFTERNOON, Eric and I were wandering upstream along the banks of the river at Alpha, when suddenly we heard a sound that chilled us to the marrow. It came from about 200 yards to our left, passed high over our heads, and died away about 200 yards to our right. Almost immediately it was repeated, not once but again and again until the air was full of it. It sounded almost exactly like the neighing of a horse, but carried over our heads through the air. It seemed to us a ghostlike and haunted wail.

We were so frightened that we raced for home, and were lucky not to break a leg or a neck in the many ant-bear or spring-hare holes.

When we told Father of our frightening experience, he said that he also had often heard the same weird sound, but that he had never been able to discover what caused it. Jafta, however, stoutly maintained that what we had heard was the voice of the 'ghost of the marshes'!

One moonlight evening a little after this, we heard the same cries coming from the vlei below the homestead, and Father called Eric and me to go with him and try to find out what made them. We had just got to the edge of the vlei when the 'neighing' started again, coming apparently from about a hundred yards to our left, passing some distance in front of us, and dying away about a hundred yards to the right. It all took only a few seconds. The cry came again, this time much closer than before, and passed almost directly over our heads, and we caught a momentary glimpse of something hurtling through the air, whether a bat or a bird we could not see.

This was the only occasion on which we actually saw what we later learned the Voortrekkers had called the 'nightmare-bird'. If it actually was a bird, it must have been one of the frequenters of vleis and swamps. But unlike snipe and other vlei-birds,

61

which are so slow-moving that they can be brought down by the kieries of the herdboys, it moved like a streak. Then, too, it was never heard by day. Is it possible that it 'goes into top gear' during the night only, and that the neighing sound is made by its tail-feathers, as the tail-feathers of some other birds make a drumming noise, or is it perhaps a mating call?

One of the older inhabitants of the Free State has told me that years ago the nightmare-bird could be heard almost any night in the vleis round about his farmhouse, and that the cries were in fact so usual as almost to go unnoticed. But no one, as far as he knew, had ever seen the owner of the voice. He believed it belonged to some kind of snipe, since it was never heard far from marshes or vleis.

There was a widespread belief amongst the Voortrekkers, and even up to recent times, that the mysterious knots in the manes of horses were the work of the 'nightmare-bird', a belief that grew up no doubt because the cry of the creature is so much like the neighing of a horse.

Late one summer's afternoon I was sitting on a spur of the Mensvretersberg, or Cannibal Mountain, absently watching the shadows from the peaks above gradually creeping out on the plain below, when I was suddenly startled by what sounded like a whirlwind sweeping over me. I instantly turned round and was just in time to see the tail-end of a swarm of finches making straight for some karee-trees in the kloof below.

I had been screened by a three or four foot high broom-bush, and as I was sitting perfectly still the birds had apparently not noticed me and must have passed only a foot or two above my head. They were returning from their feeding-grounds in the corn-lands, and as this was the first of so many and such large swarms, I wondered how they could possibly all find sleeping-quarters in the karee-trees and reedbeds beyond.

As they passed, I was particularly struck by something I had often noticed before, the perfect way they kept their even distances in flight. Except for those on the outsides, each bird was ringed round above, below, and on both sides by others, and their wing-tips could not have been more than a couple of inches apart.

All at once it occurred to me to make an experiment. What, I thought, would happen if they were suddenly frightened while in full flight? So when the next large swarm that came my way passed over me I jumped up right in their path. If I had expected to see many collisions as a result of this 'alarm', I was disappointed. They passed at such speed that it was of course impossible to see exactly what happened, but in that fraction of a second the whole swarm had risen to a level at least twenty feet above their original line of flight, and yet, as they surged forward, they still maintained the same perfectly spaced formation.

They had hardly disappeared in the direction of the trees for which they were making, when a totally unlooked-for incident occurred, for which a grey harrier hawk was responsible. A new swarm was passing thirty yards to my right, when the hawk swept down on them from a peak high above us. The hawk fell with incredible swiftness on to the swarm, but the finches had already observed him and had suddenly accelerated. Then, as he was in the act of striking, they dived downwards, at the same time dividing neatly into two groups which allowed the hawk to pass between them. At the moment they divided, they appeared to stop dead in their tracks, flashed back the way they had come, and joined up into their original formation, all in the twinkling of an eye.

The sheltering trees were 300 yards away, and no sooner had the swarm turned than their enemy again attacked. This time, they rose straight up, compelling the harrier to pass underneath, and always they kept perfect formation.

When they reached the shelter of the trees, they dived for cover and disappeared as if they had never been, leaving the disappointed hawk spiralling slowly to heights from which he could launch fresh attacks on victims less difficult to secure.

One day, while we were fishing for yellow-fish in the Vaal River, a kiewietjie was involved in an incident that deserves mention here.

We had run short of bait and could find no crabs, so we decided to shoot a bird or two with our airgun, as yellow-fish will sometimes take this bait greedily in running water. There were no small birds in sight, but eventually we saw a number of kiewietjies standing in the open veld. By circling gradually closer, we came up to within about forty yards of them, and as they were now showing signs of restlessness Eric decided to shoot.

The small pellet struck with a dull thud, and immediately the wounded bird tried to fly off. Finding however that his wing-tip was broken, he immediately pretended complete unconcern. He walked quietly away from us, all the time pecking on the ground for all the world as though he were bent only on feeding, and as though nothing unusual had happened. Seeing this, his companions returned and settled about him.

Our first thought had been to close in and finish off the wounded bird, but what had just happened interested us so much that we stayed where we were. No sooner had his mates settled round about him than the wounded bird ran between them, crouching low and keeping his friends more or less in line with us; and in a very short time he had disappeared into the thick grass in an old ploughed land.

The whole manoeuvre, from the time the bird was struck, was carried out so skilfully that it reminded one of the movements of a quick-witted rugby centre bluffing his way through the opposition.

We did our best to find the bird, but without success. We went off, however, feeling that not much harm had been done, as his injury was slight; and this feeling somewhat lessened our sense of guilt.

Ants: Fools and Fighters

THE ANT is no sluggard, we know, but he sometimes behaves remarkably like a fool.

I was trying to interest our Bushman Plaatjie in the ways of the ants and to impress him with the moral lessons one is supposed to learn from ants in order to be wise.

It was midsummer and long strings of grey ants were hurrying along the footpaths, and for some reason they were extremely aggressive. Plaatjie was barefooted, and the insects tormented him so much as we followed a footpath, that he sought temporary safety from them on top of a small termite-heap. As I had shoes on, I was not troubled by them, so I leaned against the ant-hill with easy negligence.

We could see the ants passing to and from their nest a few yards from the footpath, and I hoped to impress Plaatjie with the team spirit that ants can display when there is work to be done. For this purpose I had brought along some dead flies, a cricket, and several grasshoppers.

I first dropped a fly in the path, and it was immediately seized by one of the ants and carried triumphantly away. That of course was a one-man job. But I wanted Plaatjie to see what they would do when a concerted effort was needed, and so I dropped a large cricket about a yard away from the path, know-ing perfectly well that before long one of the scouts would discover it.

I was not disappointed. The scout tested the weight thoroughly, pulling first this way then that, and when he was satisfied he made a bee-line for the crowd in the footpath.

The moment he gave his 'message', there was great excite-ment and a number of the ants rushed round in circles before hurrying back along his spoor. But try as they would they could not move the cricket. It was not only because it was heavy, but I had purposely wedged it in between short grass-stems, so as to make it difficult to dislodge.

Plaatjie now became really interested. 'Why they not bite grass away?' he asked.

And I added, 'Yes, or bite the cricket into small pieces and carry them to the nest separately?'

'Look,' said Plaatjie suddenly. 'Some he pulling this way, and some that—they very stupid.' This was perfectly true; and I must admit that I have since then seen them doing the same sort of thing dozens of times.

Whether or not the ant is 'wise' can be argued about, but there can be no denying that he is a great fighter.

Nowhere are such fierce battles waged as in the insect world, whether between single individuals or entire communities. When communities or colonies are involved, these battles may well be said to be the last word in total warfare, so determined is each side in its efforts to annihilate the other. But there are other encounters which closely resemble guerilla warfare, such as I saw one day in the Bushveld of the northern Transvaal.

I sat watching a colony of termites at work. I was particularly interested in the soldiers guarding the 'gates', or entrance holes, and tested them in various ways, even to the extent of allowing one large-headed chap to bite a forefinger. After this I felt convinced that no enemy could ever enter their sanctuary, and when my brother Willie, who is a keen naturalist, told me that the commando ants—those terrible blue-black quarter-inch-long marauders—sometimes raided them, I was sceptical.

As the nest of this colony of termites was only about 150 yards from the homestead, I could study them almost daily. It must have been a fortnight later that one day a commando ant scout slowly and stealthily stole up to the termite nest, and I watched his every movement with the greatest interest. He seemed to be nosing out a trail much as a dog would, and I wondered how near to the gates he would approach.

Presently, when he was still some yards away, he found himself approaching a worker on the outward journey, and at once came to a dead stop. The worker passed within about three inches of him and went his way. Thereupon, the scout moved slowly and carefully towards the nest again, got on to a leaf above what he evidently knew to be a run, and remained there motionless for perhaps half a minute while termites going to and from the nest almost rubbed against him.

He was now only about two feet from the 'gates', and I was wondering what he would do next, when, having evidently made up his mind, he went quickly forward, stopped a moment, and then as if he had seen enough, turned round in his tracks and went straight back the way he had come.

I remembered what my brother Willie had said, so I followed this scout, keeping well in the rear in order not to frighten him.

After having gone about a hundred yards, he entered underbrush so dense and thorny that I was forced to stop; but I knew, of course, that if he were to lead a regiment back to the nest he would have to retrace his path, and so I went home for a quick cup of tea.

On my return I waited for about ten minutes at the spot where I had last seen the scout, when it struck me that the regiment might have already have passed, and I hurried towards the nest. There, however, I found everything normal.

On going back to where the scout had disappeared, I heard a soft sound like the crackling of dry leaves, and at that moment the advance guard of the blue-black army came into view. They marched in such compact formation that they looked like a black blotch of shade against a background of sunlight. They appeared to be in no hurry, moving forward very deliberately. But there was something decidedly sinister in their appearance, and on several occasions when I got too close to them to their liking there came from their ranks a warning 'si-si-si' sound not unlike that produced by wind blowing against tightly drawn thin twine.

They advanced steadily like an inexorable fate, and when they got to about ten yards from the termite nest, I went to my usual look-out, from which I had a clear view of the entrance holes.

I could not see what happened to the termites that crossed their line of march, but not a single one arrived at the 'gates' to give a warning, and the advance guard took the sentries completely by surprise. There was no time to block the entrance holes, and in a few seconds the black horde was streaming into the nest without meeting any opposition. The termite guards at the 'gates' always take up positions somewhat inside the openings, so I could not see what happened, but presumably they were immediately annihilated by the attackers.

Before long, the raiders were emerging, each grasping in its jaws two, three, or even four of their hapless victims, and in an astonishingly brief time the whole regiment was on the return march with the spoils of war.

The most exciting fight that I ever witnessed was one between red and grey ants, in a bare spot about four yards square, on the bank of a spruit. I have no idea what caused the disagreement for I came upon the scene when the fight was in full swing.

The common grey ant is generally good tempered, but at a certain time, towards the end of the summer, it turns vicious. The rarer red ant is a much slower mover, but exceedingly tough in a quarrel. It has a hard body, and its bite is very painful and slightly poisonous.

The nests of the two swarms were about ten yards apart, and the two sides had met half-way to settle their differences. At dusk the combatants retired to their respective nests, but at sunrise the battle started again with each side throwing in fresh reserves. On the second day the fight was obviously going in favour of the reds, and it seemed only a question of time before they would finish off their brave but less tough opponents; on the third day, however, something totally unexpected decided the matter—a colony of 'sugar' ants joined in the fray.

These insects are large, soft-looking and long-legged, and their almost transparent stomachs, slow movements, and mild appearance, all go to suggest that they are not capable of fighting or even defending themselves; but looks never proved more deceptive.

For reasons known only to themselves they came in on the side of the grey ants, just in the nick of time, and they gave such a good account of themselves that the result was not long in doubt. With the aid of their long legs they were able to hold their opponents at a safe distance, grasp them by the middle, and with one bite slice them in two.

A few hours later, not a single red ant was left alive. Many of the victorious greys, however, were still struggling to relieve themselves of the heads of their opponents, that even in death were firmly grasping their legs. This was a problem that even their friends the sugar ants could not solve, and by degrees the greys retired, till at last only the remains of those that had perished littered the battlefield.

Mambas

NO SNAKE has aroused as much interest and alarm as the African black mamba. It is extremely shy and secretive, and even that famous student of snake life, the late Frederick William Fitzsimons, formerly curator of the Port Elizabeth Snake Park, admitted that he knew very little about the early life-history and the habits of the mamba, although he had had ample opportunities of studying these reptiles in Zululand.

When I read this, I realized that I myself had never seen a black mamba under seven and a half feet in length, although I had shot a number and encountered many more in the Bushveld.

Some people are of the opinion that the green and the black mamba are one and the same snake, that they live mostly in trees till they reach a length of between seven and eight feet, and that they then turn black, or rather slate-blue, when they end their arboreal existence, and come down to live on the ground. As green mambas rarely if ever reach a length of eight feet, this at first seemed to me a likely theory, but since green mambas have, as far as I know, never been seen in the northern Transvaal, where there are nevertheless a great many black ones, I rejected it. Quite recently, in an old deserted ant-hill, my brother Eric found a nest of very young black mambas, one or one and a half feet in length, but even he, although he lives in mamba country and is a very keen observer, has not seen a half-grown black mamba.

What makes a study of mambas so difficult is that these shy and extremely dangerous snakes never breed in captivity.

Scientists tell us that snakes have no ears, and that they only feel vibrations through their bodies. Be that as it may, there is no doubt that they 'hear' exceedingly well. Over a long number of years I have certainly never encountered a mamba when I was moving noisily through the bush, and beaters on a hunt in the bush feel perfectly safe even in the thickest cover as long as they can keep up a good racket, for they know that any mambas in the vicinity will vanish into their holes long before the advancing line is in sight.

But it was something my brother Willie told me of, that had happened on his farm, that made me realize how acute their hearing must be. A pair of beautiful greenish starlings had built a nest high up on the roof of his house. The parent birds were at it all day carrying insects to satisfy their ever-hungry young ones, who kept up a continuous chirping for food. The cries of the babies were audible to the human ear for a distance of only about 150 yards, yet mambas were attracted to the house, some from a distance of at least half a mile from their holes at the base of the cliffs of the 'snake spot', and in the course of a few weeks Willie killed no fewer than four, of nine to ten feet in length, trying to scale the wall. After the young birds had learned to fly, and they and their parents had taken their departure, there were no more snake visitors.

When I first went to the Bushveld, I had the feeling that I might meet a mamba at every turn, but nothing happened, and eventually I began to doubt whether I should ever see one. Then one day my brother-in-law and I were riding down a steep and winding footpath that became so difficult to negotiate that eventually we dismounted and led our horses. I was in front carrying our only fire-arm, a shotgun. We had just crossed a small mountain stream, and had breasted a sharp rise on the farther side, when out of the corner of my eye I caught a glimpse of something about ten yards to our left. I looked and saw a gleaming coil lying on a flat rock. I realized at once that it was a snake, but as I had seen so many during the course of my life it neither surprised nor frightened me. I was stooping to pick up a stone to pelt it when it suddenly raised its head to about four feet above the coils, and eyed me steadily and intently. I had never before seen anything in the snake world that looked half so sinister, and I now realized that at last I was looking at a mamba.

As I was slowly raising the shotgun one of the horses shook its bridle, and instantly the snake uncoiled itself and moved quickly in my direction. The long grass that came up almost to where I was standing hid it for a moment, but the next instant it flashed so close past me that it actually touched the gun. It did not attempt to strike, probably because I stood perfectly still.

Although I had heard much of the speed of these creatures, I had no idea they could move so swiftly and silently. This all happened so suddenly that I had no time to think or to feel frightened, but as it was gliding over a stone about twenty yards away I sprayed it with a charge of shot, and broke its back. Not five yards beyond, under a rock, we found the hiding-place for which it had been making.

When we measured the mamba we found it to be just over ten feet. It had appeared to be twice as long when it passed us, and from this and subsequent experiences I have come to the conclusion that the fifteen-footers of which we so often read probably seemed longer than they actually were because of their speed. I myself have never measured any above ten and a half feet but Eric killed one of exactly twelve feet.

There have also been many fanciful accounts of the top speed of a mamba; I should consider it as between fifteen and twenty miles an hour. I know one small grass-snake called *labitsi*, or lightning, that is much faster. Actually the speed of the mamba varies according to the nature of the ground. It can travel fastest in rather broken ground, where the surface is not slippery and allows for good purchase; stunted bush is ideal in this respect. That it can outpace a horse is pure nonsense. It gains maximum speed almost immediately after starting, but it tires quickly. It never goes far away from its home, and so does not need to maintain a high speed for more than twenty or thirty yards at a time.

My brother Eric once came upon a pair of mambas during the mating season. He was making his way down the small Brandboontjies River on the look-out for some of his cattle that had strayed, when he heard a rustling on the bank above him inside a thick clump of small trees and scrub. Thinking that it might be caused by one of the missing cattle, he went up to look. As he approached, the noise ceased, and he stood for a moment peering through the branches.

There were no cattle to be seen, but just then he heard a hiss close by, and about five yards away he saw the head of a mamba raised above the scrub, to be joined immediately by another a foot farther off. He was carrying no fire-arm of any sort, not even a stone or a stick.

Uncertain whether he had been seen by the snakes or not, he at first stood perfectly still. He quickly changed his mind, however, when the foremost one began to broaden its neck almost after the manner of a cobra, while at the same time it raised itself higher and higher. Turning in his tracks, he ran off at full speed and jumped down a six-foot bank, not stopping until he had reached a clearing about thirty yards away.

In spite of his fright of a moment before, he was now so overcome with curiosity that he returned slowly towards the place where he had seen them. Suddenly both snakes raised their heads out of a hole in the bank only a couple of yards from where he had descended it. Ordinarily they would have retreated down their

73

hole at his approach, but now they raised themselves to nearly half their length, hissed loudly, broadened their necks as though they were being inflated with a bicycle pump, and gave every indication of being ready to attack if he came any closer. Greatly regretting the fact that he had no fire-arm, he had no choice but to withdraw silently and leave them severely alone.

It may, for all I know, have been one of these snakes that met its fate a little distance from that very spot some time later, when the owner of the farm and a gang of labourers were busy making a dam.

One of the labourers, who came from a kraal somewhere down the Great Letaba River, was a real 'wild man' and not able to do any ordinary farm work, so he was employed as a watchman to guard the implements used in the construction of the dam. For sleeping-quarters he built himsef a rough hut out of twigs and tambookie-grass. It was so carelessly constructed that one could see right through it from several angles. According to his standards, however, it was a first-class house.

One night he was awakened by hearing something moving about the hut, and thinking it was merely a mouse, he did not trouble to investigate. He lay awake for a time and presently heard a mouse squeak close at hand. He realized that it was in trouble, and being inquisitive he went towards the door. In doing so, he stepped on the tail of a snake, which wriggled itself free and fled through the moonlight towards a hole about five yards away from the hut. Having dealt with snakes all his life, he concluded it was not a mamba or it would have bitten him, and he was very much surprised when, on the following morning, he found a large mamba sunning itself almost on top of the snake hole.

I happened to arrive at the farm that day, and the farmer asked me to accompany him to the dam. When we reached it the watchman was busy setting a snare over the hole, and he proceeded to give us an account of what had happened. The type of snare he was setting is widely used by the tribesmen for catching small game of all sorts, but I had never before heard of its being employed to catch a snake. It consists of a strong, springy sapling planted upright and then bent down to within about a foot of the ground. There it is fastened by a plaited twine with a noose at the opposite end, so constructed that it holds the bent sapling in position till something puts a foot or a head through it. On being released the sapling jerks the victim from the ground to hang dangling in the air.

I had my doubts about whether this snare would work with a snake, but after the midday meal the 'wild man' came to the house to announce that the snake was *fetsi*, meaning finished or dead. Arrived at the spot, we found a nine-foot mamba stone-dead, hanging by its neck from the noose.

This was certainly the snake of the previous night, and the only reason we could think of for its not having bitten the watchman when he trod on its tail was that it had the mouse in its jaws at the time. Mambas are very seldom on the move at night, and the cool night air may also have made it lethargic. On this occasion it had been forced to look for food by night, as there were too many human beings about during the day-time.

This method of catching mambas, which I found strange enough, was not quite as curious as my brother Frederick's way of killing them. He baited a strong fish-hook with a mouse, and left it, attached to a hand-line, at the entrance of a mamba's hole. A monster of ten and a half feet took the bait.

In January 1926 my brother Eric was returning on foot to his farm, on the lower slopes of one of the spurs of the mountains of Modjadje.

It was very sultry and he felt tired after a long afternoon of following up guinea-fowl, so that when a young fellow named Botha overtook him on a bicycle Eric heartily agreed with him that they should take turns at cycling. One was to cycle for about a mile, and then wait for the other to catch up before starting the next stretch on foot. When it came to Botha's turn to cycle, the track ran straight though a steep dip. It could be seen clearly from where they stood, and appeared to be perfectly safe for a fast run.

Botha was about half-way down the slope when Eric noticed what looked liked a stick lying across the path, just beyond the bottom of the dip. He had not noticed it before and now realized that, at the speed Botha was travelling, the obstruction might easily upset him.

Hardly had this thought crossed his mind when he noticed that the object had moved, and he realized that it was no stick at all but a snake. Botha did not notice the reptile until he was almost on top of it. There was nothing to do but run over it, and the next instant, man, machine, and snake were entangled in a widly struggling mass. Botha came down heavily, and the bicycle and the snake both passed over him.

The snake then slithered down the bank and into a hole underneath the roots of a large dead tree. Eric, who had come on to the scene by this time, fired a charge of shot into the hole, which proved to be quite shallow. He then fished out the snake with a stick and found it was a mamba of just on nine feet.

Botha got off with nothing worse than cuts and bruises, for the snake had struck at the iron frame of the machine instead of at the man, and had shattered its poison fangs, as Eric discovered after he killed it.

My brother Willie lives about four miles out of Duiwelskloof in the northern Transvaal; and about a mile and a half to the east as the crow flies is my own farm.

The old homestead stands on level ground inside a kloof of enchanting beauty, some 3,000 feet up from the foot of the mountain, and from the front stoep the eye looks directly on to a dark ridge across the divide, some six miles to the east, where lives the mysterious and legendary Modjadje, or Rain Queen, of whom so much has been heard and written. It was in this old house that Rider Haggard let his imagination run riot; here he got the ideas for such books as She and Jess and The People of the Mist.

I remember clearly the first time we travelled, in the warm moisture-laden air, to the house; slowly up and up along the twisting and turning mountain drive, crossing in every little kloof a noisy mountain stream, and hearing all around the drowsy 'zings' of the countless cicadas, and below us an everchanging view of the beautiful bush-country.

The owner of the farm at that time was Frederick Ferreira, who was, even then, an old man; and as he had arrived in those parts when he was a youngster of 17, he was a living encyclopedia on the subject of the Bushveld.

The morning after our arrival, we were drinking coffee on the front stoep as the sun rose over the Rain Queen's ridge, and the old man, seeing how obsessed I was both with the beauty of my new surroundings, and with the prospect of hunting, proceeded to caution me about the possible dangers. Leopards, he said, were rare, and the nearest big game about thirty miles away, but what I should beware of was a wounded bush-pig or a bushbuck ram.

'And above all,' he said, 'be always on your guard against snakes. Forget all the nonsense you have read about mambas attacking on sight, or Natives walking about the footpaths with flat stones or pots of hot porridge on their heads; but remember that a frightened mamba fleeing to its hide-out will strike at anything coming in its way. And while you look ahead, glance down continually for the lazy puff-adder or the spiteful cobra at your feet. With practice one learns to do these things automatically.'

Most of this advice had been instilled into me since boyhood; but it was his reference to mambas that most effectually brought me down to earth.

Yet as I stood looking at the park-like country, with its noble wild-fig-trees, the dark-green luscious foliage of the deeper kloofs, and the brilliant colours of many flowering trees, I found it hard to believe that a terrifying death could be lurking among so much beauty.

The next day I had my first sight of a snake in that Eden. I had gone out with my gun and was waiting, on a fairly high, flat rock in a clearing, for any pig, bushbuck, or duiker that the beaters might drive towards me, when on the other side of the rock I saw a part of a snake. The head and tail were hidden in the grass and scrub, and about two feet of glassy scales reflected the sun about two yards away. I was wearing rubber-soled shoes and had come stealthily along a footpath, so that the snake was unaware of my presence. I could not see what kind it was, but remained quite still so as to disturb neither it nor any possible game.

Presently, I could hear by the excited barking of the dogs that something had been put up, and a moment later I had the mortification of seeing a number of bush-pigs crossing a clearing a good 200 yards away from me. I glanced down and saw that the snake was still in the same position.

Several times the dogs gave tongue again, but the diminuendo in their voices plainly told that the quarry had broken back. The beaters quietened down as they neared the edge of the bush, and I was considering what I should do when a duiker came past me at breakneck speed.

The gun flew to my shoulder, and as the buck collapsed I looked down. The grass was being disturbed close to a big boulder about ten yards away; the snake had vanished. Whether or not it really was a mamba, as Mr Ferreira thought, I had been put on my guard.

Since then I have killed about a dozen mambas, and I have wondered at times whether they are really as dangerous as they are made out to be. An encounter I had about two years ago, however, convinced me that the price of safety is eternal vigilance, no matter how beautiful the scenery might be.

It was on my brother's farm, where I had promised his herd-boys to shoot dassies for them in the kranses of hill ranges. The country is wild and rugged, and the dense vegetation at the foot of the kranses, chiefly thorn, provides excellent cover for wild pig, bushbuck, and duiker, to say nothing of every kind of snake;

and it was into this rugged tangle that I penetrated, not only to shoot dassies but also to ferret out bee-hives and shoot for the pot some of my brother's own domestic goats that had gone wild and were as difficult to hunt as any wild animal.

I was working my way up a sort of divide between the kranses with my brother's ridgeback bitch going before me, when suddenly she stopped, cocked her ears, and bristled all over. I peered ahead but could see nothing to account for this. Looking at her again, I saw that she had scented something that alarmed her. The movements of her head, sideways and up and down, clearly showed this. Then suddenly from the right side of the divide, which here narrowed to about two yards, and not more than five feet ahead of where I was standing, there shot out a black streak, like a huge watch-spring, into the matted brush on the left side. I recognized it at once as a mamba, and although by this time I had lost much of my dread of these snakes, I felt a distinct weakness at the knees when I realized how easily it could have struck at me, had the dog not given warning and stopped me.

Another day, one of the herdboys and I were laboriously climbing up a steep slope towards the kranses, when I suggested that we look for dassies at the place we called the 'snake spot', because of the large python and the many other snakes that inhabited it. My companion was not a bit keen, and made the excuse that he had to herd his goats farther along the comparatively open ground where there were some small *mapoko* mealie-lands. I told him to keep more or less level with me till we had moved to a point beyond the 'snake spot', while I tried to shoot something for him as we advanced.

I had not been able to find the dog when we left home, and I carried only my ·22 rifle to shoot dassies. At the first rocks I was presented with several easy chances, and was able to shoot two large dassies. I tied their hind-legs together and proceeded cautiously on my way.

By this time the herdboy was about a hundred yards below me and his shouting at his charges kept me informed of his whereabouts. For my part, I whistled softly to him at intervals.

Suddenly he called out 'Motoori! (Mamba!)' and warned me that one was coming my way from where the goats had disturbed it. I at once dropped the dassies and stood at the ready, listening intently. I knew that if it was a mamba it would come up towards the kranses and that I would be more or less in the line of its flight.

I felt my heartbeats quickening and I blamed myself for not having brought the shotgun.

For a while, nothing happened, and then, as I heard some of the goats coming towards me, there came the unmistakable blood-chilling sound of a snake slithering over the ground.

Where I was standing, a fairly open space extended for about ten yards behind me, up to the foot of the krans, but in front the trees shut out the view so effectively that I could see no more than about three or four yards before me. Dry leaves were lying thickly scattered everywhere under the trees, and since I had frequently observed that snakes find it difficult to move quickly over short smooth grass or dry leaves, I stepped forward quickly, thinking that the snake was still about twenty yards off.

I stopped at the edge of a perpendicular drop of about four feet, balancing myself against the bole of a medium-sized tree, and waited with beating heart and nerves on the stretch. The herdboy kept calling to me from a safe distance, and once I heard him say, 'O bolaile podi (He has killed a goat)', but I remained perfectly still.

Then, as some of the other goats, unaware of the danger, came in my direction again, I once more heard that dragging sound over the leaves, and I leaned forward slightly so as to be better able to see through the trees. Immediately, I found myself so close to a mamba in the act of lifting itself above the four-foot drop or step, that its head was not more than five feet away from my gun. The snake stopped and remained still. The gun was at my shoulder, but pointing about a yard to the right of the mamba, and I would have to move it that distance to be able to fire. We maintained a rigid silence, facing each other, and I was filled with fear as I looked at its cold eyes and flickering tongue. Then, turning on my axis as it were, slowly, infinitely slowly, I gradually edged the point of my weapon in the direction of the snake; but before I could align my sights it sank from view behind the step, and slithered back the way it had come.

Just then, however, a number of goats crashed through the undergrowth, and turning in its tracks the mamba once more made straight for me.

My mind worked with the swiftness of my danger, and I instantly realized two things: that this time the mamba would make straight for its hide-out; and that I was directly in its way. So I did not lose an instant in putting some yards between myself and its path.

Luckily, as I have said, the slippery leaves prevented it from moving fast, and by the time it cleared the step I was at the ready with my ·22. It went straight on towards the krans, scattering leaves in its wake, and as from this new angle a number of small trees obstructed my view I despaired of getting a shot. A few yards from the foot of the krans, however, it lifted its head to slither through the fork of a small tree, and knowing that the rest of its body must follow, I took a snap shot at the fork. To my immense relief I saw the contortions and twistings that told that a vital part had been struck. The head part, however, was still full of fight, and I had to put another bullet through its neck.

I called to the herdboy, but nothing would induce him to come up to me, and he only joined me again when I had cleared the tangle and got on to more open ground, carrying the two dassies and dragging a ten-foot-two-inch mamba, to the head of which I had tied a creeper.

Part Three
DASSIE

I acquire a dog

I HAVE never been for long without a dog of my own except for the years I spent in Europe as a student, and even there I had a number of dog friends.

Some years ago I wanted another dog, but I was not sure just what kind and breed I should get. For one thing, it would have to be a hunter, for the wild pigs were becoming very troublesome in the lands adjoining the bush on our farm in the Bushveld of the northern Transvaal, and it takes a good dog to spoor and help drive them out of the dense cover in which they lie up during the day. They are extremely pugnacious, and a large, slow or dull-witted animal will stand no chance against them. An intelligent dog of medium size that can move around quickly to avoid their swift rushes and murderous tusks, and that has the sense not to hang on to a dangerous animal, is the only

one likely to survive for long in the bush country. If I got a good hunter, he was sure to be a good watchdog and a good playmate as well. But the dog I had in mind should also be able to adapt himself to town life, as we lived for most of the year in Bloemfontein and it was only during the school holidays that we visited our farm, which we had rented to a relative. So it was clear that I would have to make a careful choice, and that I should have to be unsparing of trouble and patience in training the dog I chose.

Someone suggested that I should pay a visit to the S.P.C.A. kennels to see if I could find what I wanted there. I went, and the din that greeted me when I entered the kennel yard was heartrending. Some of the more spirited of the animals, herded together as they were in the same narrow quarters, barked and snapped continuously, and there was a general air of tension and excitement amongst the dogs that I had never seen anywhere else. More people arrived, on the look-out for suitable dogs, and it seemed as if the animals were aware that there was a chance that someone might rescue them from this captivity. 'Please take me, I'm the dog for you!' was clearly written on every dog's face and expectant body, and my only regret was that I could not take the lot.

Suddenly my eye fell on a black dog with a white spot on his chest, and light brown spots on his forelegs, plainly a cross between a Dachshund and a bigger dog, that was eyeing me quietly but intently. He was alone in his pen and he was the only animal in the whole place who seemed to have his emotions under control. I asked the keeper why he was kept by himself, and he said that, as he was only a puppy, not more than eight months old, he did not want him to be mauled by the other dogs. The lady who brought him had said that he had caught and killed several of her neighbour's fowls, and her husband was determined to do away with him. She had cried when she left, and said that she would try to persuade her husband to let her take the dog back.

In a flash my mind was made up. Here was my dog. He was the right size, he had Dachshund blood, killing fowls meant he had the hunting instinct, and he seemed very intelligent. I went up to the wire netting and allowed him to smell my hands, and then I went off to interview his former mistress. From her I found out that he was a cross between a Doberman Pincher and a large black dachshund. The interview left us both happy, I in having found the dog I wanted, and she because she knew her 'Mickie' was in safe hands. On the way back to the kennels I decided to call him 'Dassie', however, because he looked a little like a rock rabbit.

And now, I thought, for his first intelligence test. Would he remember me, and would he realize that I was a friend ? I need have had no doubts. His wagging tail and pleased expression as he got my scent were proof enough. I took no chances, however, and fastened my tie around his neck before leading him to the car.

84

I wanted to learn something of his character as soon as possible, so I drove out far into the veld, and turned him loose while I sat down on an ant-heap. He knew by now that I was friendly, but he was plainly uneasy. He would sit on his haunches and survey the landscape for a moment, then walk about sniffing the new smells of mole, mouse and small birds, only to return again and again, whine softly, and move around restlessly.

All at once a donkey that had been standing a few hundred yards away saw him and started coming slowly towards us with his ears pricked, obviously vastly intrigued. Dassie soon spotted him, growled, and then advanced to have a closer look at the strange creature. When they were both about thirty yards from the car the donkey lowered his head and with nose almost on the ground charged straight at the unsuspecting dog. Dassie beat a retreat in such panic that he collided with the back wheel of the car, and bouncing off he scuttled up to me. I chased off the donkey, and when Dassie saw him retreating he gained new courage, and made a counter charge. Donkeys, however, are not to be trifled with, and it was all I could do to get him away from the stamping and braying animal.

I thought we had eaten nearly enough salt together for one day, and I felt that already an understanding had grown between us. Knowing that he would be thirsty by now I took him to a pool of water some distance away in a kloof. He immediately waded in and lay with the water nearly covering his back and lapped greedily. After a while I threw a stick into the water a yard beyond him and when he had retrieved and dragged it to the edge of the pool, he looked at me as if to say, 'And what must I do now?' But I did not want to force his education too quickly so I left it at that. He did not know me yet and like all young dogs was suspicious and uncertain. But I had already summed up certain of his characteristics. He had the hunting instinct, and he was wide awake and intelligent. At the same time he had a certain quiet self-assurance found in so few dogs, and last but not least he had his fair share of pluck.

But I knew that an intelligent dog can pick up bad habits as easily as good ones, and that I would have to go slowly and carefully. I looked forward with great pleasure to the task of training him but I had no illusions about the difficulties involved. All his forerunners had been specialists in certain directions. Some were merely lapdogs, some watchdogs and others hunting dogs, but my ambition, now that I had learned something of his character, was to train Dassie to be playmate, watchdog and hunter all in one.

When I arrived home my wife and daughters were at the car the moment it stopped, all eagerness to see what kind of animal I had brought home; but Dassie took scant notice of them and ran all around the yard minutely inspecting everything. I kept an eye on him, because though I was determined not to tie him up, I knew how easily he might stray at this stage. To my relief he eventually settled down quietly, no doubt satisfied in his own mind that we were friends and he could safely throw in his lot with us.

For two weeks we spoilt him to help him settle down thoroughly and get to know us well, and he became such a favourite that my wife and daughters often allowed him to accompany them when they went down town shopping. Had they gone on foot I would have had no fear of his getting lost, but I have never known a dog that could follow a motor track home, so I warned them to lock him into the car whenever they got out. One day when I arrived home, I heard to my consternation that Dassie was lost. The car window had inadvertently been left open and when my wife returned he was gone. An African standing on the pavement close to where the car was parked said he had seen the dog slowly nosing along her spoor and turning the corner of the street. They at once started looking for him, but without any result, and it was only about five hours later that I heard what had happened. I set off immediately and searched high and low, making enquiries as I went. Various people assured me they had seen a dog such as I described, sometimes hours, and sometimes only a few minutes previously; but I returned unsuccessful and crestfallen when it grew dark, wondering whether I should ever see Dassie again. The weather was very hot, and my chief concern was that he would not be able to find water.

The next morning early I resumed my search, but I could find no clues and all that day I ranged far and wide without result. Then it suddenly struck me that the day after we got him we had visited the game reserve on Naval Hill. As the wind was coming from that quarter I thought it just possible that he might have gone that way, and so as a last hope I decided to drive there. Reaching the foot of Naval Hill I came to a cul-de-sac and was about to turn back, when along a footpath that branched off to the right I saw a black creature disappearing behind a house. It was about two hundred yards away, but in that fleeting glimpse I had seen what looked uncommonly like Dassie moving away at a jog-trot. I immediately stopped the car and got out, calling Dassie's name as I ran towards the place where he had disappeared. There I found that the path branched, one track running along the foot of the hill, the other curving down into a street.

For some moments I did not know which way to turn, and then as I was about to take the path along the hill I glanced once more down the deserted street and there, about a hundred yards away, I saw Dassie. There was no mistaking that long, low body, though he stood with sagging tail and drooping ears, the very picture of misery and loneliness. He was about to move away once more when I shouted his name, and this time he stopped abruptly, raised his head and ears and looked at me uncertainly. It was only when I was about seventy yards from him that he really recognized me, and when he had got wind of me his doubts were dispelled, and his relief so boisterous and overwhelming that I found it hard to quiet him again.

Dassie's training begins

THE DANGERS THAT threaten dogs in South Africa are not only those common to all cities—traffic and poisoners and the like—but the snakes and wild animals of the veld. With the latter Dassie was to make acquaintance in due course, but my first task was to see to his schooling nearer home, and in this I had many pleasant surprises. The first thing I found out was that he was as courageous as he was sensitive and clever. He was ready at all times to fight any dog, however large or fierce, when he thought it had evil intentions towards me; but in less than a week he learned to ignore dogs in the street no matter how aggressive they might be. He would brush past them with hair bristling and tail held high, but with hardly a glance in their direction.

Next came the important task of teaching him how to behave towards domestic animals and poultry. His earlier misbehaviour with the fowls was fresh in my mind and I knew how easily he could become a sheep killer, given the chance; so in good time I took him out to the farm of a friend near Bloemfontein where he could meet plenty of domestic animals. No sooner had we got there than he wanted to rush at the first fowl he saw. I shouted at him to stop, but it was only after I had shouted a second time and pinched his ears that he obeyed. Then, some moments later we passed through a large flock of fowls, geese and ducks without his making the slightest attempt to interfere with them.

When we got near the sheep he eyed them with surprise and interest, but I am sure he would have left them alone had they not got wind of him and stampeded. Seeing this he was after them like a shot, and for the first time I became really worried, as he could not hear me calling him because of the clattering of their hoofs. He caught up with a lamb that was lagging well behind, knocked it over, and then held it down with his fore-paws without hurting it, just as a good hunting dog will hold down the young of a buck, as if to mother rather than kill it. But though I was somewhat relieved, I knew that even this could lead to sheep killing, a very serious matter in sheep country; so I had to call out 'No', several times, and do some more ear pinching. Later, whenever he showed any inclination to chase horses and cattle, he understood my commands so well that one word was always sufficient to bring him to heel. Indeed from this stage onwards Dassie showed himself quick and intelligent above the average.

Street behaviour was the next matter we had to attend to for Dassie was still a comparative stranger to the world outside the yard where he was born. By the time he had been with me about six weeks, however, he knew that if I put on my veld shoes, he was in for a ramble in the veld, and then his enthusiasm knew no bounds; but should I wear my town shoes and clothes, I would go off by car and he had to stay at home. He would go to the front gate and lie down on one particular patch of *kweek* grass on the side walk, the picture of misery, to watch me depart. One day, instead of using the car I decided to walk to my studio, three quarters of a mile away down town. I knew he wanted to accompany me so I told the servant to keep him in her room till I was well out of sight. I did not think he would

89

attempt after that to spoor me through the traffic and pedestrians. Judge of my surprise then, when in the midst of a lesson there was a scratch on the door, and on opening it I saw Dassie standing outside, his wagging tail, suppressed whines and pleased growls proclaiming the joy he felt at having run me to earth! Much as I admired this latest exploit I realized that it should not be repeated, as he could not spoor and watch out for traffic at the same time, so I set about teaching him not to follow me against orders. This proved to be much easier than I had expected, and soon it became unnecessary to say 'No'. I had merely to raise my arm with the palm of my hand towards him, and he understood that he had to stay.

When not bent on serious business Dassie was the most playful animal imaginable. He was particularly fond of children and whenever there were youngsters about he would join in any fun that was going. Once when some relatives were visiting us, I took the three children to a playground where there was a long slide, with steps leading to the top. I took them up the steps, and while they were sliding down I descended the way I had come, Dassie at my heels both coming and going. The moment the delighted children reached the ground they rushed round and began climbing the steps again, and Dassie promptly joined them and laboured up after them. I went to the bottom of the slide to see what he was up to, and to my astonishment I saw him gliding down in the wake of the children, with legs spread wide, as nonchalantly as if he had been doing that sort of thing all his life. After that he became so keen that he was always first at the top, impatiently waiting for the children.

Nothing amused me as much as when Dassie joined in my physical exercises. While I was doing them standing up he would sit on his haunches apparently taking no notice, but the moment I went down flat to sway or pitch he would go over on his back facing me, and roll and twist as if his life depended on it. When it was cool, however, he wanted much more vigorous exercise, so when I was too busy to take him into the veld to chase hares, we had a regular rough and tumble to keep him in condition and prevent him from getting soft and lazy. These were often such hefty tussles that anyone coming upon us might have thought Dassie was attacking me in good earnest. But I would have my turn of being the aggressor, throw him down and grab him by the throat, no doubt looking for all the world as if I were choking him. Eventually he would break away and race around the house at top speed with the tip of his tail touching the ground and his head low, sidestepping dangerous obstacles by such fractions of inches that it was dazzling to watch. In his mad career he would just brush garden implements or jump over things with an ease and speed that left one gaping. This was, of course, a glorious safety valve for his superabundant energy. But it always ended in his asserting the ultimate superiority of the one and only Dassie by attacking my legs and ankles till it really hurt and I cried for mercy. Then only would he desist and our game would come to an end. No wonder I always put on old clothes before we began our rampaging! The delight it gave Dassie was written all over him, in his heaving flanks, wide open mouth, lolling tongue and immensely pleased expression.

When I started on the serious business of training him and developing his natural gift for spooring, he regarded it all as play. First I gave the sign with my hand that he was to remain with our house boy while I went off to hide in the plantation, sometimes as much as a mile away. But following my spoor proved to be child's play to him. Then I made it more difficult by walking in circles, wading through water, jumping streams or climbing trees. Streams presented no problem to him, because he picked up my spoor on the opposite side; and following me in circles was easy. Once I waded through a shallow pan and climbed a tree from where I could see him coming. When he arrived at the water's edge he stopped, and looked around with ears cocked, and then sniffed carefully round about for the spoor. He tracked it back for about two-hundred yards, but was soon back at the water's edge. After a few moments he started slowly circling the pan with his nose close to the ground. When he got to the spot where I had come out of the water he picked up my scent and quickened his pace, and soon he was coming straight for my tree. At the foot of it he stood still, apparently at a loss. I remained perfectly still, and as I had drawn the leafy branches close to screen myself, he could not see me. Then a leaf spiralled down carrying my fresh scent, and the game was up. He gave his peculiar half growl, wagged his tail joyfully, and settled on his haunches entirely satisfied that I was up there and might as well come down. After that, climbing trees and wading through water proved perfectly useless for throwing him off the scent.

Right from the start I tried to teach him methodically, and passed on to the next step only when I felt sure that he had a good grasp of what had gone before. And now the time had come to teach him something about the art of hunting in the Free State, under conditions as close as possible to those in the Transvaal Bushveld. The only game he had encountered so far were hares and several kinds of game birds that we found on our strolls on the outskirts of the town; but now we were to try wilder places on wooded spruits and rivers. I decided to use our young Bushman garden boy, Kleinbooi, as a beater to draw the thick cover along the river banks, where in some places an astonishing variety of wild life is still to be found, such as jackal, otter, lynx, duiker and several kinds of game-birds and hares. By now Dassie understood my hand signs so well that I could go off and he would remain patiently with Kleinbooi to drive the game towards me. At first Kleinbooi no sooner moved in my direction than he would bound off on my spoor, but after I had stopped him several times before he came right up to me, pinched his ear and told him to go back, he kept pace with the boy while they zigzagged through the cover. At first he did not know the meaning of all these exercises, and it was not till I had shot down a guinea-fowl which he had flushed that he suddenly understood what it was all about.

After this if he went too far ahead of the beater, to where he could see me at my post, all I had to do was to lift my hand and he would slink back to join the advancing beater again. If I wanted him to go just ahead of me, all I had to do was to say '*voor* (ahead)', and he would immediately trot off to zigzag about twenty yards ahead of me, and when I said '*agter* (behind)' he would promptly come to heel.

Having got him to this stage, I decided to see if I could teach him to drive game towards me without the aid of a beater, although I had never heard of a dog doing this. I selected a patch of bush and scrub about thirty by twenty yards, took him to one end and told him to sit down, while I went to the other end and called, '*Soek hom!* (look for him!)'. He promptly made straight for me, however, and I had to try other tactics. I threw a pebble into the thick cover about fifteen yards from where we stood, and as he rushed after it and disappeared into the matted undergrowth I slunk back to my former post on the opposite side. Then luck again played into my hands for he put up a hare which I was able to bowl over as it raced past me. The battle was, of course, far from won as yet, and a good deal of ear pinching and stern commanding were still necessary. But by dint of much patience and constant repetition, he at last learned this, the most difficult lesson I ever taught him.

Curiously enough there was one apparently simple thing I could never teach him to do, and that was to bring things he had retrieved right up to me. He would swim with waterfowl up to the water's edge and leave them there, and if anything fell into thick cover he would carry it to an open place and then drop it, seemingly quite satisfied that he had done his part of the job. I could never decide whether this was due to the fact that he had no retriever blood, or whether my teaching was at fault.

We go camping

DASSIE AND I must have slept out of doors on the banks of rivers scores of times, at week-ends and in the holidays, in winter and summer, and he knew as well as I did what was in the offing when I cleaned a gun or handled a fishing-rod. We chose only the wildest and most inaccessible places, the kind of places where fish and game are very rarely disturbed and where one had much more opportunity of studying unspoiled wild life than in more civilized parts. A sail underneath, dry grass on top of it, a pillow and some blankets, this was all that I needed for bedding in summer. And I was no less happy even in the coldest winter night, provided it did not rain, thanks to a method of heating my bed an old Bushman had taught us when I was a mere youngster. He showed us how to dig a hollow from twelve to fifteen inches deep, a little longer than the length of one's body, and just wide enough to be comfortable in. At about sunset he would make a fire of grass and dry wood in it until it was thoroughly heated, then remove the ash and live coals, and cover it with dry grass or a layer of sand. A hollow heated like this will keep warmly even in the coldest weather for about twenty-four hours. With a sail beneath, and a light mattress or blankets on top of you, the heat permeating your clothes and

94

covering, you will sleep as warmly as in your own bed. And if you have to get up in the night you will hardly feel the cold because of your heated clothes. In such a bed I slept out many winter nights, and Dassie had a circular hollow, also heated, at my feet, well covered up except for his head, so that no sound should escape him.

I always slept as close to the water as possible so that I could cast my fishing-lines; and sometimes it was so cold that my dough bait froze, and I had to put it under my blankets to let it thaw. I would cast two or three lines fanwise, the rods so placed that the reels were near my head. Then even if I was fast asleep a screeching reel or Dassie's excited bark, would usually wake me at once. Practically all my largest yellow-fish have been caught this way, for at night when there is no movement on the banks, these keen-eyed and shy creatures will come in close to look for food.

There were other nights too, warm summer nights when the moon was reflected in the still water of some deep pool, suddenly broken into rings by a rising fish, or a reed swaying and quivering in the moving stream, which seemed to be perpetually carrying away the drooping fronds of the willows. With Dassie stretched on the cool white sand, and a fire crackling under my kettle, I would listen to the innumerable noises of the night—the drone of night beetles, the croaking bark of an otter, the cry of jackals, and the occasional sleepy crooning of a turtle dove, or the sudden harsh cry of a disturbed guinea-fowl.

Sometimes I invited a friend to come along with me on one of my excursions, and one summer's afternoon Cronje and I slowly snaked our way in my light delivery van through long grass, mimosa bush, wait-a-bit trees, and thick patches of undergrowth towards the banks of the Modder River, Dassie hanging out of a back window as far as he could, to miss nothing of the exciting new country we were passing through. By dint of cutting our way through bush where necessary we at last penetrated to within fifty yards of the high banks, and before long we had dumped all our stuff on a sandbank overhung by a huge willow tree, about fifteen yards from the edge of the water.

It was one of the loveliest spots I had ever seen. We were at the upper end of a pool nine miles long that flowed alternately through narrow passages and in broad reaches. For the most part it was very deep, and full of barbel, carp and yellow-fish, some very big.

My first job was to shoot something for the pot, guinea-fowl or other birds. As I had by some oversight brought along only a ·22 rifle, flying shots were almost out of the question, and because of the rank grass and underbrush it would be equally difficult to spot birds standing or running. However, as the sun was about to set I saw a guinea-fowl settling on the top of a tall mimosa, and as guinea-fowl are extremely wary birds I had to stalk it with the utmost care, keeping behind trees and avoiding stepping on dry twigs. Dassie followed like a ghost, and so close on my heels that ever so often I felt his nose touching my legs, or I might not have known that he was there. I was only about ten yards from an overhanging branch from behind which I had hoped to get a shot, when Dassie suddenly sprang past and in front of me with hair bristling and growling fiercely. I stopped in my tracks and saw a large puffadder lying coiled up and ready to strike right in front of me, with Dassie standing almost over it. I was so close to it that I was able to put a bullet through its head even as Dassie sprang aside. Then only did I realize that I was wearing shorts, certainly the first time that I had been guilty of such an indiscretion in snake country. Had Dassie not intervened, another step would have brought me to within striking distance of the deadly creature and it would have buried its half-inch fangs in a bare leg. A few moments earlier I had had eyes only for the guinea-fowl I was about to shoot, but now I had only one desire, to get out of the tangled undergrowth in which we were standing as soon as possible and on to more open ground away from the banks.

By this time the sun had set and I had to return to camp empty-handed despite the wealth of birds round about. It was a real disappointment, not only because a spitted guinea-fowl or pheasant is a great delicacy, but because we needed the guts for bait for the night, since dough bait is very often removed by the small fry long before a big fish can take it.

By this time an almost full moon was rising and as Cronje had already fixed up our beds, and started a fire half under the willow, I was able to cast my lines before we settled down to eat. Then, when the smell of grilling chops filled the air, and the kettle was coming to the boil, a guinea-fowl, disturbed by something on the opposite bank came flying over to our tree and settled on a branch almost directly overhead. The ·22 was close to Cronje's hand and I whispered to him to try a shot, in spite of the bad light. The next moment we heard the thud of a striking bullet, and the bird fell like a stone. To our consternation it landed right on our fire place, upsetting the kettle, and sending the sparks flying in all directions, and before we could rescue it half its feather had been burnt away. However, we lost no time in rescuing it, glad to have got our roasting bird and our bait after all.

We had finished our meal and were busy sipping our mugs of coffee when, fifty yards away, one of Cronje's reels screeched, and by the speed at which it was turning I knew that something big had been hooked. With the light tackle we were in the habit of using it needed much experience and skill to land a big fish, but Cronje was expert at the art of playing big catches, and after about five minutes of reeling in and giving line a twelve pound yellow-fish was landed. This success put us in the best of spirits, since we had had no bites for a long time, so we celebrated the occasion with another round of coffee. But not another bite could we raise in spite of alternating meat and dough bait. Eventually we decided to turn in after we had moved our rods closer to our beds and carefully set each reel to allow just the right strain, so that the fish should not snap the line.

It gives one a curious feeling to realize that although the bait is lying deep down at the bottom of the pool yet should a fish pick it up the warning screech will sound only a few feet away from one's head; and there is a feeling of expectancy that is hardly conducive to sleep. But in the end we slept soundly, knowing that the warning ratchet or Dassie's bark would wake us.

As small fish had been nibbling off our dough and only barbel were taking the meat, I tried to think of some tougher bait, and suddenly I hit on the idea of some green mealies we had brought with us. I threaded two of my hooks fully with mealie pips, which I knew the small fishes at any rate would find very difficult to remove, and hoped they would remain on the hook till big yellow-fish came along—though of course there was the possibility that yellow-fish might not eat mealie pips!

At about two o'clock Dassie woke me. For a moment all was quiet and then one of my reels played out again. The moment I lifted the rod I knew that something heavy was at the other end. In trying to control the fast revolving reel my hand got so badly burnt that I had to use my sleeve for braking. After taking about fifty yards of line the fish suddenly turned in towards our side of the pool and I was able to retrieve some much needed line.

By this time I knew it was a big large-mouth yellow-fish by the undulating way it progressed when on the run, and I felt the full thrill of the angler's tensest moments, when his tackle is light and the quarry so strong that the utmost alertness and concentration are required to allow just sufficient strain on the line to tire the fish without allowing it to snap. By degrees the pace slackened, but several times when I thought the fish was nearing its end there was a sudden rush towards deep water and I had to start all over again.

At long last my doughty opponent broke water about four yards from the bank, but it was by no means as good as landed. I have never yet used gaff or net, believing that the yellow-fish should be treated with the dignity it deserves; and only by lifting it to dry land with a forefinger inserted in its gills can the angler have the satisfaction of knowing that he has really won, having given it a sporting chance to get away to the very last. Cronje had never before seen a nineteen pound yellow fish, and his astonishment was equalled only by his look of sceptical surprise when I told him it had been taken on a few mealie pips. We landed a carp and several other yellows during the night, but towards daybreak we became so tired and sleepy that had it not been for Dassie's warning barks, we might not have heard our reels going. Strangely enough, although Dassie always woke us when a reel screeched, he took not the slightest interest in the landing of our catches.

Later on in the morning, with Dassie following at his heels, Cronje stole carefully along the high banks that overhang the pool, on the look-out for an otter. He was anxious to get a skin, but otters are extremely shy animals, and he had no luck. On his way back to camp by a different route he found the carcase of a recently killed sheep. Near it was the spoor of a jackal, and he remembered that farmers in the vicinity had complained of their losses, and had appealed to the provincial authorities to help them exterminate jackals and lynxes. Cronje and I had neither the time nor the inclination then to join in a jackal hunt, and in any case I had no wish to try and train Dassie to hunt jackals. Being half Dachshund his legs were far too short, and jackals are so swift and elusive, that even specially trained packs of dogs often fail to run them to earth. So we put all thoughts of jackals from us, and went back to our fishing. Fate, however, had other views, and before night Dassie had upset my theories, as he was to do on more than one occasion in the future.

At about three o'clock that afternoon we heard a duiker lamb bleating piteously on the opposite side of the river, and in no time Dassie had pinpointed the spot and swum through the pool to disappear into the dense undergrowth. The distressed call of the young duiker had come from three or four hundred yards away, but as the only crossing was a quarter of a mile from our camping place, and as all was now quiet, we concluded that the lamb had escaped from its enemy or had already been killed. Minutes passed, then half an hour, and still the dog did not return, and I began to feel worried. Cronje too became uneasy, and we decided to make for the crossing and follow in the direction Dassie had taken. When we were just about to start, however, he reappeared at the spot where he had entered the tangled undergrowth and it was at once obvious that he had been involved in a fight, for he was limping and we could see blood on his forequarters. When we examined him we found that he was punctured in many places, and one foot was badly lacerated. We washed his wounds and applied iodine to those he was unable to lick himself, and bandaged his foot.

We were not prepared to let the matter rest there, so we set out to find the place where the fight had taken place. We reached the crossing which we waded through after we had taken off our trousers. We carried Dassie over the river to prevent his wounds from getting wet, and whenever the going was difficult, an easy matter as he weighed only twenty-five or thirty pounds. When we reached the spot where I judged that we had heard the duiker bleating I said, 'Dassie, look for him!' and he at once set off towards the river. Several times we were in danger of losing sight of him in the undergrowth, but the word '*Wag* (wait)' was enough to pull him up.

Suddenly, as we reached the edge of a small clearing we saw the hair bristle on his neck and back, and there lying stretched out on the ground was a male jackal, and some ten yards away the body of a half grown duiker buck. What exactly had happened we would never know and could only guess. Dog and jackal were of about the same weight; but the marks on the jackal's neck plainly told how Dassie's stranglehold had finished him off. So Dassie had after all proved himself more than the equal of a jackal; and incidentally he was the first dog I ever had that led back to a kill.

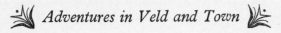

ABOUT THREE WEEKS after Dassie had killed the jackal the two of us found ourselves at the same camping spot again. It was about 3 p.m. I had cast my fishing-lines, and was resting in the shade of the willow, when the dog lifted his nose into the breeze that was coming from the direction of the crossing. I knew by the way he was lifting and lowering his head that he was scenting some animal, probably five or six hundred yards away. On a number of occasions when he acted in this fashion I had gone the way he indicated and had found a fresh spoor or had actually come on the animal itself.

I did not take much notice now, and a few minutes later I went back to the van to bring down the rest of our stuff, and forgot all about Dassie. It was not until almost an hour later that I suddenly realized he was not with me. For about five minutes I called at intervals hoping every moment that I would see his sturdy black body and wagging tail. But when he failed to put in an appearance I was thoroughly alarmed, and I hurried to the top of the bank so that my voice might carry further over the veld. Between shouts I held my breath to listen intently for any sound of his whereabouts, but there was no reply. Suddenly there came a faint cry of something in distress, and when it was repeated I was certain that it was a dog's. It seemed to come from far upstream where the mimosas merged with the darker shadows of the river banks. My heart beat loud with fear but I struggled to be quiet and listen once more. There it was again. I ran down to the willow, threw off my jacket and sprinted along the foot of the bank so fast that before long my breath was coming in gasps. The going was unbelievably rough. Deep dongas and ruts, dense undergrowth massed around large willow stumps, and trees and creepers impeded me so much that in places I had to worm my way around impassable barriers. To avoid a deep donga I climbed to the top of the bank, and once more with pounding heart I tried to listen. For a moment all was still and then clearer and stronger than before came the distressed cry, heartrending now. For about a hundred yards I ran through a comparatively open space, and I was about to brush past a large tree when my foot caught in a root, and I came down so heavily that I was completely winded and for some moments I was unable to move. Then as I got up I felt a sharp pain in my right calf, and looking down I saw blood trickling down onto my foot. A splinter of dry root had cut a deep gash in my leg; but as soon as I had made certain that no veins were cut I struggled on.

Presently I found myself following a faint footpath that ran parallel with the river, and every time I stopped for an instant I could hear the cry more clearly. The footpath became more distinct and turned down towards the bed of the river, and then as I emerged from among some tall trees I saw Dassie on a sand-spit at the crossing, lying on his side. When he saw me he struggled to a half-sitting position, but he was obviously caught in some kind of trap, and completely helpless. Then I remember nothing till I knelt down beside him. His leg was caught in a steel trap that had been set for jackals, but was big enough to have held a leopard. The double spring was so strong that in my exhausted state I could not, however hard I tried, release the poor animal.

Putting all my strength into it, I could manage one spring, but I found it impossible to press down both sides simultaneously. I was frantic with the hoarse cries of the dog in my ears, and in despair I shouted at the top of my voice; but I soon realized that the chances of anyone hearing me were almost nil, as the nearest farmhouse was two miles away and the farmer and his shepherd seldom came down here. The cruel teeth of the trap had crushed through bone and muscle, and I had visions of having to carry him to the farm, trap and all. Suddenly I caught sight of a heavy log about ten yards away, and gathering him up painfully, trap and all, I carried him to the log, so that I might weigh down the point of the log on to one spring, and force the other one down with my weight. By this time what with my bleeding leg and Dassie's wound, and blood from a bite that the dog in his agony had aimed at the trap but that caught my hand instead, we were literally covered with blood and dirt. By an almost miraculous piece of luck the log was not too heavy for me to lift, and yet heavy enough to press down one spring, and almost before I could believe it Dassie was free. I realized afterwards that at that moment I was more desperately tired than I had ever been before, and I think the same was true of Dassie for he hobbled along painfully till he reached the water and then sank down to drink as if he would never stop. How long we remained there I do not know; but eventually I carried him all the way to the van, circling well out from the banks into more open country.

It was easy to imagine what had happened. He had got the scent of the jackal from our camping place, chased it till it crossed the river at the shallow, and landed in the trap that had been set for the marauder. It is common knowledge how clever jackals are at avoiding traps, and no doubt this one knew exactly where the danger spot was. When I took Dassie to a veterinary surgeon the next day he found that some bones had been broken. I needed quite a lot of patching up myself, and when we reached home my family hardly knew to whom to attend first, the man or the dog.

Dassie's leg mended soon, but it was a couple of months before we could go camping again. Meanwhile he was not idle, but learned a number of lessons that stood him in good stead later on. Various of my acquaintances kept asking why, if he was so clever, could Dassie not do any of the usual parlour tricks like sitting up and balancing bits of food on his nose. I tried to explain that stuffing a dog's head with worthless things makes it all the more difficult to teach him anything really worth while. But after a close friend had thrown out such a challenge I decided to teach him at least one trick, and eventually I taught him one that baffled everyone who saw it.

When we had a number of guests I would come out dressed for a ramble in the veld, which they all knew was Dassie's signal for a walk—and it was always obvious that he was quivering to go. Yet when I set off, without saying a word to him, instead of following me he would sit down in his peculiar, half sideways manner, and watch hungrily as I turned the corner. After a little I would return. Then I would go out again, and this time Dassie would frisk with delight, and trot ahead of me as he always did on a stroll. We would repeat and reverse my leave-takings in whatever order my friends suggested, and Dassie would play his part correctly every time. Every one would be watching for a secret sign but nobody succeeded in discovering any, and even when I told them to watch my hands carefully they were still none the wiser.

What happened was this: if as I started moving forwards I clasped and unclasped my right hand two or three times, it was the sign that Dassie could come along; but if I made no movement with my hand he had to stay. When I had started teaching him this trick, I actually told him to come or stay, and simultaneously made the sign very clearly about ten times; but as soon as he grasped my meaning I gradually stopped giving the word, lessened the number of movements and made them slighter, till eventually a mere flick of the fingers was all that was needed for our purpose. In the end he came to know perfectly well that we were playing a game, and entering into the spirit of it, sat waiting for me to return with a roguish and expectant look on his face.

It sometimes happened that I was away from home for a day or two, and I always had complete confidence in Dassie's ability to guard my family. He had an almost uncanny capacity for knowing when anyone came on to our premises, no matter how stealthily. One evening we were at supper, listening to the news on the radio and Dassie was lying stretched out on the floor, when he suddenly rose in the tense, expectant way peculiar to him. I got up and went as quietly as I could into the kitchen, and opened the door that led out into the orchard. Dassie slipped out like a shadow, and a few moments later he started barking amongst the peach trees, in a way that indicated that he had cornered or treed something. I found him standing up against the bole of the tallest peach tree, peering into the branches above, where before long I discovered two terrified schoolboys keeping as far out of harm's way as possible. I persuaded them to come down, filled their pockets with peaches, and allowed them to go, knowing quite well that they would never again attempt to help themselves to our peaches at night.

There was rather a different story one cold winter's evening when I sat writing with Dassie lying in front of the radiator close to my feet. It was about ten o'clock when Dassie suddenly lifted his head, and then remained perfectly still as if listening intently. As there had been a number of robberies in our area recently, I got up and opened the door quietly, and he slipped out into the dark night. Seconds later I heard a terrific commotion, sounds as of blows striking the ground, wood splintering, half suppressed voices, and a dog's muffled growls and grunts. I ran for a torch and by the time I returned the scuffle was coming from next to the hawthorn hedge that divided our yard from a neighbour's, but by this time the intruder had somehow forced his way through and I could not see what was happening on the other side. Just then Dassie gave a yelp of pain, and at the same time I heard the retreating footsteps of someone running away. The dog reappeared in the rays of my torch and to my consternation I saw that his leg was broken between the hip and the knee, and was dangling uselessly.

I rang the nearest veterinary surgeon, and was told to bring Dassie round immediately, and his leg was put in plaster. I was told that the bones would take three weeks to set, and at the same time I was warned that he would try to remove the case as soon as the leg was on the mend and started itching.

But thanks to his training, the moment I saw him biting at the case and shouted a determined 'No', he stopped and did not as much as look at it again.

Once, when my family was on an extended trip overseas. I remained behind with Plaatjie and Dassie as my sole companions. Plaatjie was a thoroughbred dachshund about one third of Dassie's size, but he made up for his want of inches and weight in aggressiveness—he loved quarrels. He soon discovered, moreover, that he could start trouble, and then watch from the side line while Dassie did battle on his behalf. At first he only picked quarrels with dogs of his own size, and these Dassie used to dispose of by butting them with his shoulder and knocking them over. But as Plaatjie grew older he gradually squared up to larger, and as he must have concluded, more interesting chaps. This landed poor Dassie in a horrid dilemma. He had early imbibed the lesson that he was not to fight other dogs unless he was himself attacked, and at the same time his whole instinct was to protect Plaatjie.

During this time I had to leave the two dogs behind for a fortnight in the care of two young schoolboy friends while I was away on a trip. When I got back I noticed that Dassie was scarred on his forequarters and head, and that the tip of one ear had a tear an inch long. In answer to my questions the boys told with great zest how Dassie had been fighting dogs who had tried to interfere with Plaatjie. He had easily got the better of the smaller dogs, and then they had found other opponents for him, bigger and more worthy of his steel, so that several times he had had a tough fight.

To tell the truth I did not believe all they told me of Dassie's prowess as a fighter, but then I had never seen him in a dog fight in which he really got worked up, for as a general rule he lived at peace with the world of dogs. However I was not in the least anxious to have him involved in brawls in which he might get badly injured, so I warned the boys not to encourage him to take on dogs too heavy or strong for him.

In the block next to ours there was a large dog, a cross between a bulldog and an Alsatian, that had caused me much uneasiness. He was very fierce and although not as fit as Dassie for lack of exercise, he was strong and had the reputation of being a killer, a reputation of which his owner was inordinately proud. Whenever we passed, the dog rushed out at Dassie, but as soon as we stood still, as we always did, his courage deserted him and he turned round slowly and retired to the house. Then one day when I returned from shopping I found both dogs in a bad way. Plaatjie, with a deep gash in his shoulder, was walking on three legs, and Dassie had a number of wounds and was bedraggled, tired and subdued. The boys looked very worried, no doubt expecting a good scolding for what had happened, and by degrees I got from them a full account of the whole affair.

They were taking a stroll with the dogs when the killer spotted them. Plaatjie had already cleared the low wall and was dashing across the lawn to meet him when he was knocked off his feet and then Dassie promptly fastened on to the dog's ear. He turned on Dassie, and immediately their muzzles were interlocked, and the big dog was so strong that he dragged Dassie all over the place. By this time his owner was on the scene, no doubt feeling sure of a speedy end to the fight, but neither animal would release its hold. Meanwhile the boys were standing helplessly by, afraid to interfere because they might be bitten themselves. They begged the man to separate the animals before Dassie was killed, but his only answer was, 'Let them fight it out.'

Suddenly the dogs stood apart for the fraction of a second and then Dassie was knocked clean off his feet. But resorting to a favourite stratagem he fastened on to the other's forepaw, the most sensitive part of any dog's anatomy, and the animal at once began to howl and struggle to free itself. But Dassie held on grimly. The owner was now so beside himself that he aimed a kick at Dassie, but fortunately missed him, and his next door neighbour, who had been watching the fight, and whose fox terrier had nearly been killed by his dog, stepped in between them and said furiously, 'No, let them fight. Don't separate them now that your dog is getting the worst of it!'

Suddenly the big dog managed to free his paw and like a flash he got a hold on Dassie's throat, and Dassie could not shake him off. He was being slowly strangled and it seemed to the onlookers that nothing could save him. But now at last fitness began to tell against want of exercise and over-eating, for with a sudden desperate wrench Dassie managed to free himself and in a twinkling had fastened on to the same foot. Then, feeling that his opponent was weakening, he seized his chance and in turn got a grip on the other's throat. In a short time its sides were heaving and its tongue lolling out when its owner managed to wrench it free. It had had enough, and with what wind it had left it fled towards the back of the house with Dassie in hot pursuit. Then it crept under a bedstead in a back room, and there the boys and the two men found Dassie, in an uncontrollable rage, slashing and jumping back in one tearing action, as he did when fighting wild animals. They caught hold of him before he could damage the dog any further and took him home. And never after, when we passed the house, did the big dog show any desire to try conclusions with Dassie again.

We went on a visit one day to some friends in the northern Free State who did large-scale poultry farming. As Dassie and I were much more interested in a near-by spruit where there was excellent fishing and guinea-fowl shooting, we saw very little of the hens for the first few days. The runs and sheds were in a bluegum plantation, about five hundred yards from the farm-house. There was on the farm a large eight-months-old Boer-hound called Wagter with whom Dassie, an affable soul, soon became friendly. It was tied up most of the time and I warned my friends that large dogs that are tied up can become a danger, as they have no chance of gaining the experience they need to know their rightful place in the comunity. So as an experiment we had his chain removed and began teaching him to guard the fowls. We first would take him into the plantation so that he could get accustomed to the sight and presence of so many birds, but I thought it wise to hold him on a leash.

Next day I repeated the experiment, and as on neither day had he shown any particular interest in the fowls, I thought it was safe to turn him loose in the runs. The moment he was freed, however, he made for the nearest hen and began chasing it. Dassie was standing just outside the wire netting fence, and when he saw this he rushed to the gate, jumped through an opening three feet from the ground, reached Wagter just as he was pinning down the fowl, and fastening on to one of his ears shook with might and main. Had the Boerhound been older he would never have tolerated such an indignity, but being young, and taken completely by surprise he let go the bird and made for the gate.

The next day I took him to the runs again, but this time Dassie accompanied us, and it was easy to see that although Wagter was sorely tempted to give chase Dassie's presence exerted a restraining influence and he left the fowls alone. Dassie himself had long since been taught not to molest fowls; and when he heard me caution Wagter and pinch his ears, he understood perfectly, and felt it his duty to join in the lesson.

Dassie gets lost

I ONCE LENT my dog to someone, a thing I shall never do again. Not that Dassie did not understand the position in an instinctive way, because always, if I wanted him to accompany or remain with anyone, all I had to do was to say, 'Dassie, go,' and point to the person he should follow, or else say, 'Dassie, stay,' and raise a palm towards him and he would always obey. He was never entirely happy about it but he knew that all would be well if he obeyed. And so when Willie and his friend Jan, who had arrived from Rhodesia to stay with us for a couple of days before going on to Cape Town, wanted a day's shooting on the Modder River, about thirty miles away, I agreed to let Dassie go with them as I was unable to do so myself. They were complete strangers to Dassie, but I knew that he would be of real help to them.

The farm they were going to belonged to a relative of Willie's, and although I knew more or less where it was I had never been there myself, nor had Dassie. Their car was one of the old type

of sedans fitted with small windows, and from where he sat Dassie could not see out, and had no idea where they were heading for.

They had a most successful day and their bag included half a dozen guinea-fowls, a spurwinged goose, several Egyptian geese, and some partridges and hares. When the sun set they decided to wait till it was dark, so as to be able to shoot spring hares with the aid of a bull's eye lantern. This was a sport that Dassie knew nothing about as on principle I was against this kind of hunting, and so although he must have seen and smelt hundreds of spring hares, he had always ignored them. But soon after they had started he went off on a spoor, and though he was heard to bark furiously, the hunters did not pay much attention to it.

A little later they decided to move on to a spot about two miles away, and forgot all about Dassie, and it was only when they were about to return to Bloemfontein that they realized that he was not with them. Greatly perturbed they went back to where they had seen him last, stopping every now and then to call him. After driving about and searching for another two hours, and nearly getting lost themselves, they came to the conclusion that Dassie must have taken the road back to the city, the more readily as they had heard so much about his unusual spooring ability. So at last they decided to return to town, hoping they might find him some where on the way. What they did not know was that no dog can follow the spoor of a motor-car once the tracks have mingled with those of other cars. In addition Dassie had not been able to see out of the window on the outward journey, and this was all new and unknown territory to him. In spite of a large bag, it was a very subdued pair of hunters who returned to the city, for they had seen nothing of Dassie on the way back. They were full of his praise, what he had done during the day, and how intelligent he was; and they were so much upset at having lost him that in spite of our own anxiety we had to console them, and assure them that Dassie would find his way back in due time, something we would have been very glad to be sure of ourselves.

We persuaded them that all would be well, and that they could continue their journey next morning as they had planned. It was a relief to me to see them go as my one urgent desire was to set off for the Modder River and look for Dassie. From what I had gathered from Willie and Jan of their movements, it seemed clear to me that Dassie must really be lost, since he could easily have covered the distance home in about three hours, and it was now about fourteen since he had last been seen.

I had no difficulty in finding their tracks after they had left the main road, and at a place where the soft soil made spooring easy I stopped the car and walked on examining every inch of the way, and I found that Dassie had covered the ground here three or four times. As it was useless to look for tracks on the main road I decided to call at all the farms along the road and to speak to every one I saw on the way.

Before setting off again, I tried to put myself in Dassie's place. As he had not been able to see, and had no idea in which direction the town lay, he might have crossed the bridge and followed the road to Boshof. Or he might have followed the course of the river, either up or down, in either case going further away from Bloemfontein. I was sure that he would not make friends with anyone unless he was completely exhausted. What worried me most was the question of water. It was very dry at this time, and apart from the river, the only water to be had was in boreholes or cement dams on the farms, with walls too high to allow a dog to reach the water. Cattle troughs were nearly always empty after the livestock and poultry had been watered.

The nearest farm to the point where the car had left the main road was about three miles away, so I went there first. The farmer said that on the previous evening he and his wife had heard a dog howling far away in the direction of the river, but they had gone inside and had forgotten about it. There were some native huts about three miles away on a rise near the river, so I set out for them on foot, as the ground was too rough for a car. When I got there, however, they were deserted except for a number of piccanins, who fled into one of the huts when they saw me, so there was nothing for it but to go back to my car.

I continued my search, calling at every farm, tramping miles in the hot sun, questioning everyone I met, man or woman, black or white. But no one had seen the dog. I felt no hunger, but at last I had to ask for water at a native hut; but even as I lifted the beaker to my lips I felt I had no right to drink while Dassie was suffering the pangs of thirst.

I arrived home that night in as dejected a state of mind as I have ever been in. It was not only that I knew Dassie was probably wandering around hungry and thirsty and tired, but what distressed me most was the thought of his misery and loneliness. For four years we had been inseparable, day and night. I lay awake for a long time picturing him jog-trotting across the veld, his ears low and his tail almost touching the ground, testing the breeze every now and then for a familiar scent.

Next day I crossed the bridge and continued my search along the Boshof road. Again I called at every farm and spoke to everyone I met, and I went out of my way to visit all the native huts, as the most likely to yield any information. And it was in one of these, about twelve miles from the river, that a woman gave the first news of him. On the previous day a dog, like the one I described, had come to their huts, and she had found it trying to get at a little water, all that remained in the bottom of an earthen pot with a narrow opening. She could see by the collar round his neck that he belonged to white people, so she knew he must be lost. She was on the point of fetching water at the borehole half a mile away, and intended giving him some as soon as she got back, but by the time she returned he had vanished, and she did not see him again. So all the rest of that day I continued my search, until at sunset I was so weary and footsore that I had, for the time being at least, to admit defeat.

The next day, the fourth on which Dassie was missing, was a repetition of the previous two. But there had been a change in the wind. On the first day it had come from the east, and on the next two days it had changed to north and north-west, and now on the fourth day it had swung round to south. I had noticed these changes and now I realized that if only Dassie had not wandered too far, his delicate sense of smell might pick up something in the wind that would make him turn his course towards Bloemfontein. It was therefore with a faint spark of hope that I turned into our driveway that evening. But when my wife and daughter came out to meet me I knew at once by their faces that Dassie had not come home.

I was nearly exhausted as a result of my long hours in the hot sun and my anxiety, and my wife urged me to give up the search, especially as we had put advertisements in all the papers. But I was determined to carry on, and fell asleep with my plans made for the next day. I woke from a deep sleep at first cock-crow, and wondered, as I had done so many times during the last few days, where Dassie could be at this moment. My imagination was conjuring up a host of possibilities, mostly of such a gloomy nature that I found it impossible to stay in bed any longer, when suddenly a dog barked at the front door, and almost simultaneously I heard my daughter rush down the passage leading to the lounge. I don't know who reached the electric light switch first, but the next minute Dassie stood in the open doorway, and then, instead of standing up against our knees as he always did to welcome us, he sat down just inside the door, lifted his head, and cried as I have never heard a dog cry before or since. Before I could make a move my daughter had picked him up in her arms, her eyes full of tears, and carried him into our bedroom.

Soon he was lapping a plate of milk as if he would never stop, and when he had eaten as much meat as we dared give him in his starved condition, we were able to examine him thoroughly. He was so thin that the bones stood out on his shoulder blades, ribs and hips, as if they would pierce the skin. He stank of the putrid meat he had picked up, and he was so covered with dust that his colour had turned to a dirty brown. To judge by the condition of his feet he had been following hard gravelly roads, and must have covered enormous distances, for in places the soles of his feet were quite worn through and raw.

We washed and doctored his feet, then made a bed for him in a corner of the room of blankets folded into a cosy nest, and there he slept and was fed for four days. It was at least a week before he could move about freely again, but no king could have received greater care and attention than were lavished on Dassie in that time.

We are caught in a storm

TO BE A SUCCESSFUL angler of fresh-water fish in South Africa, the first essential is to be able to forecast weather conditions for some days ahead as accurately as possible. It is for this reason that many fishermen are expert 'weather prophets'. They seem to know instinctively the direction of the wind from day to day, and what changes there are likely to be in the next couple of days. They become so proficient in this art that they can feel the prevailing conditions even although they are laid up indoors. Actually it is not really an instinctive feeling as in birds or animals, but an acquired art, born of much experience and observation.

The way in which fishes react to weather conditions has always astonished me. Time and again it happens that all the signs are completely favourable for angling and yet not a bite can be raised, and then invariably during the next couple of days, or even after the lapse of a week there has been a severe

hail-storm in the vicinity or in the catchment areas of the river or dam. Storms, and especially hail-storms, often churn the water up to such a muddy condition that the fishes die in thousands because of the mud that fills up their gills and chokes them. How they know so far in advance what the weather is going to be it is impossible to say; but it is quite certain that they are extremely sensitive to coming changes outside their element, and that they appear to know that an empty stomach lessens the danger of choking in muddy water.

A town dweller, however, cannot pick and choose his days, and will sometimes have to go out in search of sport against his better judgment. And it was with such mixed feeling that I set out one day accompanied by Dassie for a distant spot on the Modder River. Cronje was to take us to the river by car and return to Bloemfontein, and after three days come back for us. There was something in the air that gave both of us a peculiar sense of uneasiness, the sort of feeling, no doubt, that sometimes causes hawks and swallows to fly for distant cover for no apparent reason. The sun was shining brightly, but a warm north wind was steadily and easily flowing over the countryside, carrying with it a moisture-laden haze, and far to the south some clouds showed their heads. But they were a hundred miles away, and we threw off our uneasiness.

The river was low, and after Cronje had set us down on the bank I waded knee-deep through twenty-five yards of water to an island, three hundred yards long, from the lower end of which one had a good chance of catching yellow-fish. Having cast my lines I decided to spend the night on the island, and I had to make several trips across the stream to bring over my blankets, kettle and other paraphernalia, leaving a ground sail in which I had wrapped the ·22 rifle and my greatcoat in the shelter of a bush.

I had just settled down when I got a bite and immediately realized that I had hooked something powerful. A long fight ensued and while I was playing the fish I felt sorry that Cronje was not with me to share the fun. When I landed it, a beautiful fifteen pounder, I discovered that it had been foulhooked underneath a fin and that this plus the strong stream had aided its powerful rushes. A little later I saw a very large yellow-fish flash past downstream in a rapid, but after that, in spite of seemingly perfect conditions, I did not have another bite. I felt pretty sure, however, that the big ones would be on the bite some time during the night, so when the sun set I prepared to get some sleep as the moon would rise late. Dassie, who had thoroughly explored our island, stretched out on the sand and I followed suit by lying down on my blankets, and being very tired after a long and active day, I was sound asleep long before the moon rose behind the mimosas on the eastern bank.

Suddenly I was roused by a loud bark from Dassie, and I automatically rose to a half sitting position to listen for a screeching reel. The next moment I wondered if I was still dreaming, for only about a foot below me a raging torrent was sweeping by in the moonlight, and as I looked, large logs and debris of every kind was being carried along on its flood. I realized in a flash that these were the advance waters of a much greater mass to follow. The river had risen so suddenly that even Dassie was taken unawares, or he would have warned me sooner. I made a faint attempt to reel in the lines, but they were already fouled, and a few seconds later the water was lapping against my blankets. I abandoned everything after that, and hurriedly threw off all my clothes except my trousers and shirt. My shoes I threw as hard as I could over to the bank, and had the satisfaction of hearing first one and then the other fall with a thud on dry ground.

As there were sure to be rapids and whirlpools further down in the deeper part of the stream, I made my way as far up the island as possible before trusting myself to the madly tumbling waters. Though I swam half against the current, I was carried downstream so rapidly that a bump against a tree-stump or a rock would probably have injured me badly; but my luck held, though several times I had to struggle for breath after having been forced below the surface or rolled over by the strength of the stream. Suddenly I found myself in a backwater, and realized that I was at the top end of a deep pool where we have often fished; but the level ground on which we had stood was now entirely submerged, and the bank above it so steep and slippery that I had to hang on to a projecting root I had managed to catch hold of, to get my breath back.

I was still holding on, wondering what to do next, when I heard a snort close by, and turning my head I saw Dassie, whom I had quite forgotten in my own struggles. He must have been carried down further than I, for he was working his way laboriously towards me, and trying to find a landing place. I let go the root, and gradually made my way, now swimming, now seeking a purchase in the bank with fingers or toes, to a place where I had often landed my catches. Here too the level ground had disappeared beneath a steadily strengthening torrent, and the high bank was steep and slippery. But I put out every ounce of my remaining strength to crawl and slither up it, at the same time helping Dassie along, until I fell exhausted in the mud at the top.

I had only the shirt and trousers I stood in, and had I known how they would hamper my movements, I should have shed them before I started. The moon was still shining but dark clouds were massed along the horizon to south and west, and lightning flashed almost continuously in the south, where the catchment area of the Modder River lay. The first thing I did was to try and recover my shoes, and I was just in time as one was already half covered by the rising waters. The coat, sail and ·22 were luckily still safe and dry under their bush, and luckiest of all was the fact that I had put an extra box of matches in my coat pocket, a precaution I had learned by hard experience in the past.

So now we had a ground sail, eight feet by six, a military coat, a ·22 rifle and fourteen cartridges, and a box of matches. My shirt and trousers were wet and muddy, but fortunately it was fairly warm. The nearest farm I knew to be about five miles away, and in two day's time Cronje would come to this place to fetch us. Rain, and plenty of it, was coming up fast.

There were several clumps of *taaibos* near by, a bush that sends out tough and pliable shoots in a circle from the root, leaving an open space in the middle. I chose one that grew on a sandy rise high above the level of the water, and sheltered on the south and west by mimosa trees. Having broken off some of the smaller shoots inside the circle to enlarge it, I found I could scoop a hollow in the sand for a bed for the two of us, and I pulled out several handfuls of grass to line it with, cutting my bare hands a good deal in the process. Then I drew all the shoots together and tied them at the top with strands of wild tulip to form the skeleton of a hut, and spread the sail on top for a roof, tying it down with more tulip strands. I took off my sodden shirt and trousers and put on my coat, and lit a fire of the dry wood that lay around, and then I gathered some more tulips to reinforce our shelter as the rain was not far off, and I knew that the wind that precedes such a rainstorm is often of hurricane force.

In due course the wind struck from the west, and drove large scattered drops of rain with the force of hail stones against our sail, and between the ribs of our shelter. Soon after the storm broke in earnest. The wind howled against the mimosas and the *taaibos* brakes, and shook our hut, and the air about us was full of whistles, shrieks, creaking and shuddering blows, that seemed to batter against our ears. Dassie and I sat pressed close together, crouching under the greatcoat. The lightning was so severe that most of the time I could see as clearly as by day, and Dassie, always nervous when there was thunder and lightning, was shivering like a leaf, though I covered his head and ears as much as I could.

Our little hut stood up remarkably, for though the wind drove spray right through, the direct rain was kept off us by the sail, and in a lull in the wind we turned our grass over, dry side up. It was growing colder, but I spread the coat over us, and Dassie pressed close up against my back, and we were soon fairly warm and comfortable.

Suddenly, however, the wind veered from west to south, and blew with frantic strength, and the rain came down in such torrents that the farmers on the Modder River later spoke of it as a cloud-burst. Though the sail still protected us from its direct fury, the rain blew into our hut, and soon the grass beneath me sloshed when I moved. So I scraped the sand into a mound, and we perched miserably on top of it. After some time I reached up and loosened the tulip strands holding the sail, and pulled it down to wrap around us, so as to keep the coat from getting soaked through. I had no idea how far off dawn was, and there was no house or rock to which we could flee for shelter. When the first force of the storm had spent itself the thunder ceased and Dassie was more at ease, but it was still raining hard. Then after what seemed to me an eternity, but must have been about an hour, the rain slackened and the air grew lighter. I thought at first this was merely the moon shining through thinning clouds, but suddenly I heard the thrice welcome call of a pheasant announcing the dawn, followed far out on the flats by that of a korhaan, and then some kelkiewyns flew crying overhead.

A feeling of exhilaration seized me, and I patted Dassie and chatted to him in my relief. Through the shoots and trees I saw patches of blue sky, and by the time the sun rose there was hardly a cloud left. Never was sunshine more welcome. My clothes and the coat were soon drying in the warm sun, and Dassie had so far forgotten his terrors of the night that he was soon following the spoor of a couple of otters that the flood-waters had driven from their homes.

The mimosas hid the river from us, but in several places the brown moving mass was flowing over the banks to form miniature lakes in the hollows, moving almost without sound. Our island must have been fifty or sixty feet below the surface, and I couldn't help wondering what would have happened if Dassie had not woken me in time.

Our immediate need, however, was food, and I set out with Dassie and my ·22 to procure some. We found several guinea-fowl which took to the trees when Dassie chased them, and which I could bring down at close range. We found too an unexpected addition to our menu in the watermelons and mealies that the river had washed down out of the lands and deposited on the bank.

The hot sun dried things in a remarkably short time, and the next two nights we slept soundly on dry grass under a clear sky; and when Cronje arrived for us we felt that all in all we had come off well from our frightening experience.

Porcupines and otters

THERE IS a popular belief in Africa that the lion and the leopard
are a hunting dog's chief enemies, but in actual fact most dogs
have such a wholesome respect for these animals that when
they encounter them, they keep well away from their fangs and
claws. The bushpig is a far greater danger, though for an
inexperienced dog the porcupine with his formidable array
of needle-sharp quills runs it a close second. The mamba and
cobra, deadly as they are, are a real menace only to stupid and
badly trained dogs. Early on in his career I had taught Dassie
not to get within striking distance of a snake. He had shown
undue interest in a cobra and I had shouted 'No', and shot
the snake before it could strike; and to imprint the lesson on
Dassie, I took it by the tail and flung it at him with such force
that it hurt him. He never got too close to snakes after that,
and I have often seen him circle round a patch of brush or a
heap of stones, his hair bristling and his body tense and alert,
not attempting to close in. A muffled bark would bring me to
where I could see the snake and dispatch it with a charge of
shot or a ·22 bullet.

Porcupines are very seldom met with during the day, being
strictly nocturnal in their habits. It takes a clever dog to
escape from an encounter with a porcupine because of the

deadly quills with which it can transfix its enemies. If it survives the first encounter or two, the painful experience will prevent an intelligent dog from making any mistakes, but in my experience it is usually the porcupine that has the best of the argument.

There was the evening when Van Rensburg's ridgeback, of whose fighting qualities he was so proud, went berserk when he surprised a porcupine in the pumpkin land. He knew nothing about porcupines, but as his master was encouraging him he made for the queer-smelling and queerer looking creature. For a moment he sparred for an opening and then rushed in, and at the same moment the porcupine turned round to receive the impact on the full battery of its quills, and the dog instantly fell dead, pierced through the heart. And on another moonlight night my cousin's two plucky fox terriers were killed in the same way.

Once in Portuguese East Africa my brother Eric shot a lion, large but old and horribly emaciated, whose paws were so riddled with porcupine quills, that it had obviously been unable to catch anything to eat, and was on the point of starvation.

My first experience of the dangers of porcupine hunting was when I and a party of youngsters of my own age were out, and our clever old bitch Molly was struck between nose and eye by a quill. It had pierced a vein and blood spouted freely. We were at a loss to know what to do till someone produced a large safety pin which we pushed through the two sides of the cut in the skin, and twisted around to form a kind of tourniquet. Every time the hold on the safety-pin was relaxed the blood spurted afresh. We could not, under the circumstances, let the dog walk, so two of us carried her while a third held fast to the safety-pin. But the third was the owner of the safety-pin and he needed his hand every now and then to hitch up his pinless trousers. The result was that all of us were soon fairly covered with blood. We did eventually manage the half mile to the house, by which time the leader's face presented such a bloody sight, that my mother nearly fainted with fright when the procession entered the lighted kitchen.

One morning when Cronje and Dassie and I were camping out, Cronje was stealing along the bank of the Riet River to shoot a game-bird or two for the pot. He was moving through a patch of underbrush beneath some tall mimosas when his foot squashed against something soft, and looking down he saw a large male lynx lying dead at his feet. It must have died a very short while before as it was warm to the touch, and fresh frothy blood stained the ground about its nose. On turning it over he saw a porcupine quill deeply embedded in its chest. Cronje expressed surprise that a lynx should try to kill an animal so totally unsuited to its mode of attack, one which under ordinary conditions it would leave severely alone, but he was answered when we discovered that one of its forepaws was broken clean away, all the claws being gone, no doubt the result of having been caught in a steel trap. Apparently it had been unable to catch its usual prey in the shape of young buck and small animals and birds, and must have grown so hungry that it tried to kill a porcupine.

At about nine o'clock that evening Cronje and I were sitting at the camp fire enjoying a mug of tea when Dassie started barking from the direction in which we had found the dead lynx. We both instantly sprang up, and even as I shouted 'Run! Porcupine!' Cronje was already speeding that way, ·22 and torch in hand. Dassie had been lying as usual on a rise about a hundred yards from the camping place, watching and listening, and we had not noticed that he had gone. The breeze that was blowing from the east must have brought the taint of something unusual to his nose, for I could hear by the quality of his bark that he had treed or cornered something.

Cronje was the first to arrive on the scene of action and found that not one but three porcupines were huddled in an oven-like hollow in the bank, their hindquarters turned to the dog, all ready to rush backwards in order to crash their quills home, should Dassie have the audacity to close in on them. My arrival had the effect of egging Dassie on, and before Cronje could do anything about it, he had rushed in to the nearest animal. There was a yelp of pain, but at almost the same moment Cronje fired point blank, killing the foremost porcupine, and the next moment the other two brushed past with Dassie in hot pursuit.

They were making for their holes, but Dassie stopped one before it had gone twenty yards. I quickly caught up with him, and to my surprise and relief I saw that he was circling so as to remain in front of the porcupine. Cronje got in another shot and a second porcupine bit the dust, but the largest one had escaped. Only then did we notice that Dassie was limping, and we saw that one quill had pierced a foreleg, another had entered close to his nose and was protruding below his ear, while a third was sticking through the muscles of his neck.

One would have imagined that a dog so pincushioned would have no fight left in him, but not so the gallant little Dassie; for when we had quickly removed the quills and turned to have a look at the dead animals he slipped away, and before long we heard him bark some distance up the river. By the time we arrived on the scene, however, the porcupine had disappeared down a deep hole. Dassie had received no further wounds, but he was obviously in a bad way, and we carried him back to camp. In order to have a good look at the porcupine we decided to carry it back too, but its extremely nauseating, gassy smell, combined with its fifty pounds of weight and the innumerable large fleas with which it was infested soon made us drop it.

There was nothing more we could do for Dassie. Once he cooled down he became stiff and sore, so we covered him up with a blanket against the chilly air and went to bed ourselves at about eleven o'clock.

Just before daybreak I woke to find Cronje sitting up listening. There was the sound of a bark and I recognized Dassie's voice in the direction of the previous evening's scuffles. I remembered then that he had seemed as cross as he was sore when we covered him up, and I guessed that the grudge he was nursing against that porcupine had proved too much to resist, and that he had gone back to settle accounts. In a few seconds we were racing over the rough ground. How long Dassie had been up there we did not know, but now all was quiet, too quiet, and fear lent me wings. When we neared the porcupine holes we stood still for a moment with our hearts beating fast, and were rewarded with a muffled noise about twenty yards to our right. Then the beam of Cronje's torch fell on a dark moving blotch, and I was quite prepared to find Dassie lying dead.

It took us some moments to find out exactly what was happening. Then we saw that the porcupine was there and so was Dassie; but he had a stranglehold on it, and had nearly torn the soft head from the body. He had learned in one painful lesson that a porcupine's business end is at its rear and not in front, and had assimilated this knowledge to such good effect that he put paid to the account of an adversary that was about twice his own weight, and bristling with weapons.

Dassie's first encounter with an otter occurred on the Modder River, about half a mile from the farm Roodeheuwel. One day soon after we had arrived, a young herdboy came running to the house with the news that Bull and Dapper were fighting something in the stream and were slowly working their way down towards a big pool. The farmer and his family were away from home, so I hurried towards the river without a weapon of any sort. There had been a drought and the stream was so shallow that except for a few pools it did not exceed two feet in depth, and was only about five yards wide.

At first there was nothing to be seen or heard, but as we were rounding a bend a great splashing and commotion reached our ears. Then we saw two large Boerhounds tackling something slightly smaller than themselves, that was twisting and rolling in the water, and was apparently too strong for them to pin down or hold. The water was growing discoloured with blood, but I soon saw that it was theirs and that they were fighting a grey otter. Before I could stop him Dassie had rushed in to join the fray. He was at a great disadvantage in the water because of his short legs, and as he closed in the otter grabbed him by the neck and pushed his head under the surface. I rushed in fully clothed, but Dassie had disappeared. The otter had been working his way skilfully down towards a deep pool, now only about a hundred yards away. Where we stood the stream had narrowed and was about four feet deep, and the Boerhounds, still full of fight, stood waiting for the otter to reappear.

At last there was a disturbance in the water at the far end of this stretch, and Dassie's tail could be seen threshing around. The hounds immediately attacked again and only then did Dassie come to the surface. He was in a bad way, and it was more my efforts than his own that enabled him to crawl to dry land again. The stream was now deepening towards the edge of the pool and I was just in time to see the otter disappearing into deep water, leaving his attackers on the bank, thoroughly bedraggled and demoralized.

It was hard to believe that an animal the size of that otter could have inflicted such terrible punishment on two dogs of the calibre of those hounds. But some time afterwards when I had an opportunity of examining an otter I had shot, I was sure that no dog however fierce and strong had any chance against one in single combat. Their bodies are entirely covered with flexible muscles of great strength, and their skins are so thick and tough that no fang can pierce them. Moreover their strong jaws and needle-sharp canine teeth are even more formidable than those of the ratel. Sometimes an inexperienced dog will try conclusions with one in deep water, but its fate is invariably a watery grave.

After this experience Dassie was far too intelligent to attack an otter without provocation. Such provocation, however, he considered had come one afternoon when I was out shooting birds. I had brought down a spurwinged goose about two hundred yards from camp, but as I wanted to go further along the river I put it in the fork of a willow tree twenty yards from the bank, intending to pick it up on my way back. When the sun was nearly setting and I was well on the way home, a strong breeze sprang up from the east and it crossed my mind that the swaying of the willow might make the bird drop to the ground. However, I knew it was too heavy to be carried away by such small fry as meercats or ordinary wild cats, and usually the larger beasts of prey wait for the dark.

Soon I was approaching the willow from the top of a high bank, but before I could begin the descent I realized that Dassie had gone down on his own some distance behind me. It was unusual for him to do this, but when I looked down towards the foot of the willow I saw the cause. A brownish animal was busily tearing at our spurwing. As it turned sideways I saw that it was a grey otter, and then I caught sight of Dassie approaching with head pushed forward, tail low, and bristling all over. He suddenly rushed at it. My shotgun flew to my shoulder, but the two animals were by then so closely locked in fight that I could not shoot for fear of hitting the dog. I slithered and stumbled down the steep bank, and as I got closer I saw that Dassie was hanging on to the side of the otter's head, probably by its ear. But now the otter was dragging him along to where there was a six foot drop into the river. I knew it was no use shouting as Dassie simply would not hear me, and as I was about to raise my gun again they tumbled off the bank.

I rushed to the edge but for the moment they had sunk from view. Then Dassie suddenly reappeared, but was quickly pulled under again, while the back of the otter showed above water. In that fraction of a second I was able to send the charge of shot into its body, and it disappeared. Dassie surfaced, choking and spluttering and chopping water and I jumped in to help him out. I fervently hoped that he would never again feel in honour bound to fight an otter.

The Bushveld at last

WE WERE GOING on holiday to our farm in the Transvaal Bushveld, and I was very divided in my mind about whether to take
Dassie along. I had lost so many dogs there—Gluck, Bosveld,
Nora, Steekbaard and others—of snake bite, diseases and injuries
got in hunting wild animals, that in the end I decided that it
would be the lesser of two evils to leave him at home in our
tried and trusted servant Paulina's care.

When we began our preparations Dassie knew there was a
journey in the offing, and watched with great excitement, and
when at last we were all packed and ready to move off he waited
eagerly to be told to get in. When he heard the unexpected and
shattering, 'Stay, Dassie,' he stood for a moment incredulous,
then he sank slowly on to his haunches, his ears sagged, his tail
curled inwards and he remained as motionless as a statue. Our
holiday was spoilt, and at home Dassie pined. And when we got
back to a tumultuous welcome from him, we decided that we
would not go without Dassie again.

There still remained the fact that he would meet many large
and dangerous animals, beasts of prey and big game and bushpigs, animals he had had no experience of in the Free State.
So I was very glad when, at about this time, he accidentally

ran foul of a large and very fierce sow on a farm in the northern Free State.

I was taking a stroll on the edge of a vlei some distance from the homestead, when, inquisitive as always, Dassie went to investigate the scent of pig that came from the long grass. I am not sure if he had ever seen a pig before, or whether he thought this was just some kind of wild animal. The pig was foraging for roots in shallow water in the long grass and her piglets were milling around her, when Dassie suddenly made his appearance.

I was standing on a dry stump, shotgun in hand, to get a better view of some wildfowl, when I saw Dassie closing in on the pigs. A piglet gave a startled grunt, and the whole bunch swung round to face the intruder, and for a moment all stood as still as stone. Dassie had also come to a stop, and with neck outstretched was sniffing the air. Suddenly the sow got wind of him and charged in a way that would have done credit to any bushpig. Dassie had no option but to run for his life; but he had first to turn round, and the water that reached to his stomach together with the long grass he stood in, slowed him up to such an extent that the sow was on him before he could as much as move a couple of yards. For a moment pig, dog and muddy spray formed one dirty blur. There was a squeal and a howl and then I saw Dassie emerging from between the pig's hind legs. He was covered with mud, horribly bedraggled and thoroughly frightened. He found himself facing the path by which he had entered, and he made such good progress down the length of it that no domesticated pig had a hope of catching him.

I felt sorry for Dassie, but the whole incident from the moment the pigs saw him till he cleared the vlei was so comical that I almost fell from my stump with laughing. I hoped that the memory of this encounter might stand him in good stead when he met with wild pigs, and was grateful he had escaped injury.

The time came at last when we took Dassie to the Bushveld, and one day my brother Eric, Dassie and I went to visit the heights of Modjadje, on the northern outposts of the Drakensberg. There stands the house, now deserted, from which Rider Haggard looked across the realm of the Rain Queen, and where he conceived the story of She-who-is-to-be-obeyed. At that time and for many years after, one looked out over a landscape where the morning mists parted to reveal valley and plain of incredible freshness and greenness, with luries calling from fern-lined kloofs, where streams cascaded ceaselessly on their way to reed-bed and river. Giant trees grew in the kloofs and on the enchanting hills—waterberry trees, marulos, kiaat and the lordly wild fig.

Now on the heights where they stood there waves a sea of eucalyptus trees as far as the eye can see. There is no morning mist, and the streams that flowed down mossy kloofs are for ever stilled. The thirsty eucalyptus trees drink up every drop of moisture. At the drift which we could only cross on horseback when the Brandboontjies River was low, children can play in the sandy bed, for it is only after exceptional rains that the springs that feed it flow. The mournful wail of the rain bird now falls on deaf ears, and Modjadje, the Rain Queen, brooding on her mysterious ridge, has lost her magic power of invoking the heavens, even over her own kraal.

Below the level of the eucalyptus plantations, where stretches of grass once separated the bushy kloofs from one another, a tangled mass of small trees and scrub has taken over, interwoven with thorny creepers so dense that one wonders how any animal can penetrate it. But this is the cover that bushbuck and wild pig frequent, and where snakes find safe retreat.

It was up the heights towards the old house that we were climbing along what had once been a road, but was now almost entirely overgrown. The going was steep and the steaming heat so oppressive that by the time we reached the old fig tree below the house we were panting for breath, although we were in hard condition. When we reached the old homestead, we found the tennis court covered with thick scrub, rose shoots were growing through the broken panes, and a colony of honey bees had built their nest beneath the flooring boards.

While Eric went to look at the outbuildings I slowly circled the house with Dassie a few yards ahead. I was wearing rubber soled shoes that made no noise on the cement, and as we got near to a corner Dassie suddenly stopped, and the hair rose along his back. Suddenly what I had taken to be a piece of creeper five yards away moved, and I saw that it was the tail end of a large snake out of sight round the corner.

I whispered, 'Staan,' and Dassie at once froze. Our only firearm, a ·22 rifle, was on the front stoep, and as I glanced back towards it I saw Eric coming to the house, and gave him a sign to walk quietly. The sign, the bristling dog, and the blue-black cord, now motionless, told him all that was necessary, and he whispered, 'Mamba! Wait, I'll fetch the rifle.'

There was now only two foot of the snake showing, too little for a shot to be of any use, and while we stood undecided it suddenly moved away, and by the time we peered around the corner nothing was to be seen of the snake. This was not surprising as the lower part of nearly the whole length of the wall was covered by a tangle of creeping roses. We felt sure that the snake had not heard us, and that it was close by, so we decided that Eric should go back round the house and stay on guard at the opposite corner while I beat the cover from my side.

I was just about to start belabouring the rose bush when Dassie, whom I had forgotten for the moment, gave a loud bark at the edge of the tennis court, twenty yards away. We both shouted at him to come back, terrified lest he should get within striking distance, but a second bark followed immediately, and simultaneously something that resembled a huge spring shot out of a dense patch of brush, and fell just short of the dog's head. He rode the thrust but he would have been much too late if the mamba had had more space in which to manoeuvre.

Eric tried to get in a shot but like a flash the snake was gone as if it had been spirited away. We knew, however, by Dassie's excitement that it was still in the brush, so after I had very sternly made him come to heel, Eric once more waylaid the snake while I tried to drive it towards him. We were both alert and tense, knowing how unpredictable mambas are in their movements.

I had just started beating when Eric flung the rifle to his shoulder and a shot rang out; but it was a clean miss and I felt very regretful that we had not taken the precaution of bringing a shot gun with us, for the speed of a mamba, coupled with its sinuous movements, makes it an extremely difficult target to hit with a rifle. Dassie could not resist the temptation to rush after the snake when it was retreating and I trembled for his safety. A second shot rang out just as the body of the snake was passing through a fork of the nearest tree, and the bullet severed the spine two feet from the head. A mamba ten feet ten inches long lay curling and twisting at our feet, a testimony to the fact that Eric is one of the finest shots that ever fired a rifle. Even though it was stone dead, Dassie had by now learned his lesson so thoroughly that he would not venture within yards of the writhing reptile.

ᘒᘓ Bushpigs ᘒᘓ

AFTER MY SISTER'S death Mooiplaats, the home of our parents, passed to me, but it was ten years before I could seriously consider restoring the old homestead. The small graveyard where our parents were buried in the shade of a marulo had been cared for and the encroaching vegetation held at bay. But the farm lay below the eucalyptus plantations, and when Eric and I went to investigate, we realized that our first task would be to interview the heads of one of the timber firms. Trees had dried up the springs from which the farm had always got its water supply, and unless we could succeed in having them removed, we should have to consider boring for water.

While these negotiations were going on, we seized the opportunity while we were there of starting a war against the bushpigs. Their numbers had increased so much, and they had grown so bold, that they had taken to foraging in broad daylight, and they were ravaging all the crops planted in the natives' gardens. The owners had appealed to us for help as they had no firearms, and though they were past masters in the art of trapping wild animals, they had learned long ago that bushpigs are much too crafty to be caught in any kind of trap. In fact they are so wily that there is a widespread native belief that if you intend hunting bushpigs you can *think* when and where you will do so, but you dare not say it out aloud.

One day the beaters were out, and I was sitting on top of a dry stump well above the scrub, waiting for their approach, when I saw a large boar in a small open patch coming towards me. As the wind was in my favour he could not possibly be aware of my presence. The beaters were still a long way off but I had high hopes that eventually he would come within range of my shot gun. He stood half concealed by a small bush, his head held sideways as if listening intently. I dared not make the slightest noise or movement, and after a time I began to suffer agonies from something sharp digging into the seat of my trousers. Not once for nearly a quarter of an hour did he flick an ear, and indeed I had never before seen any animal remain so perfectly motionless for so long a time. My seat became almost unbearable and I would have given anything to be able to shift a little or even to shout aloud; but still the boar stood there as if carved out of stone, though the beaters were now so close to him that the nearest was well within shot-gun distance.

Then, suddenly, as if his extremely subtle senses had exactly pinpointed an opening between two beaters, he streaked back the way he had come, to be swallowed by the bush, but not before he had so frightened one of the beaters that yells of terror re-echoed from fold to fold of the kloofs. By all the rules he should have passed my way, as the wildly thrashing and shouting natives were behind him; but some sure instinct may have led him to consider being driven as tantamount to being ambushed, or his ears may have told him that there were enemies in front.

Bushpigs are by nature so suspicious that often long before a hunting party has assembled at a prearranged rendezvous, though they may be a mile away in some thicket or deep kloof, they know by the sounds that something unusual is afoot. Time and time again, although experienced hunters and beaters can tell by all the signs that pigs have been there less than an hour before, yet they have vanished as though they had never been.

Their scent, sight and hearing are so keen that they are able to avoid trouble in any form more adroitly than any creature I have had experience of, not even excepting the jackal and the otter. Their streamlined bodies can move through the thickest cover at a speed that makes a bushbuck seem slow in comparison, and a large boar weighing in the neighbourhood of three hundred pounds is so compactly built and possesses such fantastic strength for its size that few beasts of prey will dare to attack it. It is on record that even lions have been killed by bushpigs. When they are wounded or cornered they are extremely ferocious, and unless one can muster a large number of beaters and experienced dogs to drive them from their strongholds it is best to leave them alone. Again and again it has happened that when we have employed only a dozen or fewer beaters we have had the mortification of seeing them move in the bush in a compact body instead of in extended order, so great is their fear of these animals. So altogether we had set ourselves a difficult task when we decided to pit our wits and experience against these redoubtable creatures.

Before taking any action against the bushpigs we had to spy out the land. We were fortunate in having the help of Jan, a middle-aged 'boy', who had been born in the vicinity and had grown up with bushpigs. He promptly set about a survey, but his first experience was far from fortunate. He was passing through a kloof covered with a thick kind of buffalo grass when his mongrel dog Bles, young and inexperienced, discovered a sow with her litter. Bles was yapping around at what seemed a safe distance when a couple of pigs attacked him from the rear. Of what happened after that Jan could not give a clear account but Bles must have been killed almost immediately. Next morning we found that the pigs had not only killed him, but had eaten every shred of flesh, leaving only the bones to mark the spot.

Our next step was to borrow every experienced dog we could, and eventually we had three native mongrels and two half-bred ridgebacks that were all reputed to be excellent pig dogs. The ridgebacks we knew were experienced and well trained, and the natives were just as confident about the capabilities of their dogs. As it is most important to be on the best of terms with hunting dogs, we housed, fed and generally made such a fuss of them that Dassie was clearly puzzled and became furiously jealous, and ready to attack the whole bunch at once. As a matter of fact my chief problem was Dassie himself, because it would be a positive cruelty to leave him behind when we sallied forth with dogs and guns, and yet he had been in the Bushveld only about a week, and knew nothing of hunting conditions here, and less of bushpigs. To let him loose to hunt them so soon would be tantamount to murdering him. When I told Eric of my difficulty, he was adamant that we should at all costs keep Dassie away from pigs for the present and I could not but agree with him.

Just then we received a letter from Cronje saying that he would arrive on the following day. This was good news, for he was a magnificent game shot, and would enjoy nothing better than joining in our campaign. Eric and Jan who knew more about pigs than Cronje and I were ever likely to learn, advised concentrating on small areas instead of trying to drive a number of kloofs and folds in one sweep. Eric said he would join the beaters and advance in the middle of the line. So next day Jan first guided Cronje and me to our positions and then hurried back to join the beaters. After that we knew that the success of the whole manoeuvre depended on our keeping as silent as the dead.

Eric, the beaters and all the dogs except Dassie, who was locked up in a rondavel, went to the starting point of their drive by a roundabout way, so as not to give the pigs any intimation of their whereabouts before the actual drive commenced, and I was sitting at the edge of a krans from where I had a splendid view of the whole terrain, and Cronje was posted some distance below me. Nowhere in the green basin, speckled with innumerable clusters of wild flowers, was there a single piece of bare earth to be seen, except right below my point of vantage, some thirty yards away, where there was a fairly open patch through which a hardly discernible game track passed. Cronje, perched on an old ant-heap, had almost as uninterrupted a view as I. Every minute now seemed like an hour as I waited for the drive to commence. All the beauty and interest of the landscape were lost on me, as I sat in tense expectancy of a breakthrough by the bushpigs.

At last the blast of Eric's whistle, and the sudden yells of a thin line of beaters broke the silence and told us that the drive was on. There were two deep kloofs between the beaters and ourselves, and the drive had started on the ridge beyond the further one; and although it was half a mile away we could clearly hear the yelling and shouting. As the line descended into the kloof the sounds gradually faded, only to rise to a gradual crescendo as the beaters worked their laborious way up the nearer ridge. Then as they began the next descent the dogs for the first time gave tongue, and from the way they were barking I could tell that they were not running on a spoor but fighting something. A little later there came the sound of a shot echoing from kloof to kloof and I knew that Eric was in action.

For some minutes after that all was quiet. So far the sounds had been easy to interpret: the dogs had brought one or more pigs to bay and Eric had been able to come up close enough for a shot. But suddenly there came a series of high pitched, repeated half yelps, half barks, that filled me with surprise and alarm, for they came unmistakably from Dassie! How Dassie had got out, and why he had followed Eric's spoor instead of mine were a mystery to me. But obviously he was alone on the spoor now, and whatever he was after was coming our way, as the barking was becoming increasingly louder. Then there was a slight rustle from the open patch below, and I saw a large boar, half shielded by brush and broadside on, standing some forty yards away. I pressed the butt end of my rifle to my shoulder but the next instant I saw Dassie coming up to him, and so close that I had to withhold my shot. Then the boar charged, and I had the intense relief and satisfaction of seeing Dassie skilfully evading his lunge before they disappeared into the brush in Cronje's direction.

After a short time I knew by the furious barking that once more the pig had stopped to fight, and almost immediately there came a yelp of pain and the report of a shot. I had to run some way along the krans to find a place where I could descend, and then I had to force my way through almost impenetrable undergrowth, the thorns half tearing my shirt from my back. But before long Cronje answered my call, and when I reached the scene of action I found him bending over Dassie, while next to them lay the dead boar.

Dassie had received a clean five-inch cut along his back, that might have been given by a butcher's knife, and there was such a flow of blood that we were at first afraid that a vein had been opened, or important sinews severed, for his hindquarters appeared to be lamed. With my jacket we improvised a hammock and then fought our way through the tangled undergrowth towards the homestead, and rendered what aid we could. Luckily Jan soon joined us and as the news of Dassie's misfortune had been relayed to him by the beaters, he had collected some roots and leaves of a medicinal plant on the way and he at once applied them to the wound, and in an astonishingly short space of time the flow of blood was stopped.

It must have been an hour later that Eric and the beaters arrived carrying a large sow that he had shot when she turned to fight the dogs, and only then could we take stock of all that had happened. The servant who had been left in charge had opened the door of Dassie's rondavel, and the dog had slipped out before he could stop him. As Cronje and I had walked round the back of the house to go to our positions, he at once picked up the spoor of Eric and the beaters, and Eric had just fired at the sow when he caught up with them. The dead animal, the strange smell, the blood, a freshly discharged cartridge case, the excitement of the beaters as they closed in to the scene of the kill, all these things must have excited Dassie tremendously and aroused all his hunting instincts; and while Eric and the beaters and the rest of the dogs were milling about the kill Dassie was nosing around, and having found the fresh spoor of the retreating boar had promptly followed it up.

Bushbuck

UNTIL HIS WOUND should have healed we could not allow Dassie to go into the bush with us, and willy-nilly he was taken back to Eric's farm, where he enjoyed no end of hero-worship, especially from the children, for the reports of his exploits had preceded him.

As we were determined to carry on the war against the pigs whenever our other duties allowed us the time to do so, I was secretly pleased that Dassie was out of action, as I was not at all sure that his first encounter would have convinced him of how dangerous it was to close with such tough enemies.

After three weeks in which we had had several hunts, more or less on the pattern of the first one, I had an even better idea of what bushpigs were really capable of. Emboldened no doubt by that first hunt and our co-operation, the mongrels and the ridgebacks had come to have a false idea of their own powers, and the result was that only one ridgeback and one mongrel were left in the field, the rest having been killed or so badly cut about and intimidated that they were of no further use for this sort of hunting. When Dassie had sufficiently recovered I brought him back to Mooiplaats, not to hunt pigs, however, but to help in ferreting out buck when we needed meat for ourselves or the boys. By this time his reputation was such that a local sportsman offered me a fantastically high price for him.

Some time after this we were all invited to join in a bushbuck hunt forty or fifty miles to the south-west of our farm. The country there was mountainous and very steep, and the slopes were covered with dense cover of brush and thorny creepers, and Eric was very dubious of Dassie's being able to follow through it. However we took him with us, and as we were laboriously inching our way through the tangled and thorny mass to a point where we intended starting the first hunt I was coming to have doubts of my own. We had about twelve dogs of various breeds all fairly large. Beside them Dassie, with his more compact body and shorter legs, looked unimpressive; and the natives who saw him for the first time were inclined to look at him pityingly and shake their heads. The other dogs had the advantage, of course, of much experience of this kind of hunting and of the difficulties of the terrain.

The organizer of the hunt, Pieter van Aardt, had been born on the mountainside, and the ease with which he moved up and down the extremely steep slopes made us envy him his leg muscles. He sent one of his drivers to take Cronje to his post, and he himself guided Eric and me to a point on the opposite side of the deep kloof. Here he posted us about two hundred yards apart, and then hurried back to assist in the drive, moving as effortlessly as if he were crossing a street. The mountain slopes here are so steep that it is a moot point whether going up or down puts the greater strain on the leg muscles. And the footpaths are covered with small round pebbles that enormously increase the difficulty of remaining on one's feet.

Dassie had simply assumed that his rightful place was with the drivers and the pack, and I had no fears of his being resented or mauled, as dogs about to start a hunt rarely think of assaulting even a stranger. Besides Pieter had promised to keep an eye on him.

Sooner than we expected we heard by the baying of the pack that they were after a bushbuck ram. For a while it seemed that the whole pack were giving tongue and Cronje and I at our different posts expected at any moment to see the antelope break cover. But a bushbuck is one of the most difficult of antelopes to drive from his stronghold, especially in cover so dense; and before long Cronje and I began to realize something of this, for the baying moved first this way then that, showing plainly that the ram was up to the age-old trick of shaking off his pursuers by again and again passing through the same dense patches. After some time it gradually became apparent that the number of dogs following him was diminishing, as one by one they gave up the chase till at last only the deep baying of one hound was heard mingling with the higher pitched and more quickly reiterated half yelps of the gallant little Dassie. Not long afterwards he alone could be heard and I experienced a thrill I shall not easily forget. We had all known that he was competing against a pack of dogs trained and operating in their own environment, and we had not dreamt that he would outlast them. But by now we could tell from the way he barked that the ram had turned to fight, and I became very much concerned for the dog's safety, for a bushbuck ram at bay is, next to a bushpig, the most dangerous antagonist any dog can encounter. Eric shared my fear and we set off without an instant's delay for the scene of action, while I fervently hoped that Dassie would keep his distance.

Pieter had taken us to our posts along game paths, and we had no idea of the difficult ground that lay between us and the kloof below. Over one stretch, when we had nearly reached our objective, it must have taken us at least a quarter of an hour to cover a hundred yards, for we got entangled in a kind of creeper we had never met before, thickly interlaced with the bushes. In addition, along its whole length it was covered with curved thorns so vicious that one marvelled how bushbuck could push through them. When we could hear Dassie barking not more than fifty yards from us, we managed to negotiate the last stretch by clearing a path with a light panga. We could hear Cronje hailing us from a distance. He was trying to work his way towards us, but soon found that he could not advance another step.

We could hear now by the change in Dassie's barking that the ram was again on the move, set off no doubt by the noise of our approach, and we listened intently for sounds of his whereabouts. Suddenly I made out a dark form moving swiftly and silently through the tangle about twenty yards from us and making towards Pieter. I tried to get in a quick shot before it passed out of my sight, but I was so tied up in the vines that it was impossible to swing the gun round in time, and Eric, who was standing next to me, did not even get a glimpse of it. Presently the animal turned again and rushed away crashing loudly through the scrub, and close on its heels, almost sailing on his belly to avoid the creepers, Dassie came into view for a moment. We knew he had winded us but he did not pause in his dash after the buck, that was trying to shake him off as it had done the other dogs. Eric and I could do nothing now but simply remain where we were, dripping with perspiration from our struggle and from the steamy heat, our shirts and trousers already almost in shreds. This way and that the chase went, with Dassie giving tongue all the time.

Then once more the sounds went in Pieter's direction and suddenly a shot rang out followed by dead silence. For the first time Dassie's spooring yelps had ceased, and one by one the natural voices of thicket and kloof reasserted themselves. Then we could hear Pieter hailing the beaters and we edged our way in his direction until we found him standing in perhaps the one open spot in the wilderness, a large bushbuck ram lying dead at his feet. He was bending down, patting and talking to Dassie who with tongue lolling and panting violently, was vigorously wagging his tail with pleasure. When he saw us Pieter shouted, 'I would give every penny I possess to own such a dog.'

Soon the foremost beaters and about half a dozen of the pack appeared on the scene. One large dog with outstretched neck was in the act of sniffing at the antelope when a black bolt shot in between his hind legs and fastened on to a foreleg. It was a case of David and Goliath. Goliath, however, was taken so utterly by surprise that he yelped with fright and pain; but the rest of the pack, seeing Dassie under one of their own number, closed in on him like an avalanche. Everyone of us, however, natives included, rushed to the rescue, and in no time the small hero was hoisted up out of harm's way, and the pack ignominiously chased off.

I found that a curved thorn had pierced the flesh of Dassie's cheek and almost penetrated his eye. We extracted it, and then, heavily laden with our quarry we slowly worked our way out of the tangle to more open ground. The natives with the prospect of a generous supply of meat before them shouted and chatted away in high glee, and vied with each other in their efforts to sing the praises of ',Ntho entsonyane (that little black thing)'.

When we were reviewing the events of the day, we all agreed that Dassie had had the advantage over the other dogs of having shorter legs and a strong compact body that enabled him to slip under obstacles instead of having to get over them. In addition he was half dachshund, and had therefore inherited the capacity for boring in, even if he had to burrow to get to the quarry. But when all that was allowed for, his spunk and tenacity had left them all far behind that day, and he had behaved magnificently.

For a long time we could hear the native beaters chattering, ejaculating and laughing around their camp fire, and though I could hardly follow the gist of their conversation, the phrase ',Ntho entsonyane' kept recurring. Meanwhile an arm's length away from where we were lying on our bed of straw, the subject of all the excitement was curled up peacefully in the folds of an old all-weather coat, seemingly asleep, but fully alert to all that was passing around him.

Leopard

AT SUNRISE THE next morning one of the native herdboys came to report that a year-old calf had been killed and partly devoured during the night. We were soon at the scene of the kill and could immediately tell from the spoor that the killer was a leopard. Dassie and some of the other dogs that had hunted on the previous day were with us, and we were standing around the dead calf considering whether there would be any sense in trying to find a leopard in the daytime in such surroundings, when I noticed that Dassie was moving away from us, nose to the ground. At first he was inching his way along but gradually he increased his pace to a slow walk. Presently he looked back at us in the manner so characteristic of him, as if to say, 'Come on. What are you waiting for?'

He had never scented a leopard before, much less seen one, and I wondered whether he was not nosing on the spoor of a buck. To make sure we followed him till he crossed a patch where the ground was soft enough to show imprints, and presently Eric's experienced eye picked out the spoor of a leopard. So that *was* what he was following.

Eric and Pieter now took over. The other dogs were kept in

147

leash in the rear and Eric and I followed immediately behind Dassie. Whenever he went too far ahead of us I said 'Stadig (slow)', and however preoccupied he was, he immediately waited for us to catch up. The going was very different from what it had been on the previous day. There were wide open spaces interspersed with patches, smaller or larger, of dense forest. Once inside these one passed into a world of giant forest trees that were ideal cover for beasts of prey.

The spoor bypassed two of these patches, and entered a third and larger one. A consultation now took place in which the beaters also joined, and it was decided that Pieter and Cronje should take up positions on the far side of the trees about four hundred yards away, and that Eric and I with Dassie held in leash should follow as stealthily as we could on the spoor. The beaters with the other dogs, also on leash, should take up positions to left and right to force the leopard to go towards the guns waiting in front. There are few animals as unpredictable as leopards, but since this one had not been wounded or annoyed we felt reasonably certain that it would not attack but would rather seek safety in flight.

As quietly as we could Eric and I, with Dassie on the spoor, moved into the glade. Coming out of the bright sunlight it was at first even gloomier than I had imagined but our eyes gradually grew accustomed to the dim light. The smell of dank decaying vegetation filled the air, and for the first time a feeling of uneasiness stole over me, and I could see that Eric felt it too. The leopard had passed over a damp surface here and Dassie was following the spoor much more easily. In a little while he stopped at the foot of a large matomi tree, and we could see that the stinging-nettles around the bole had been disturbed and flattened. We peered carefully into the foliage above but seeing nothing we passed on.

We estimated that we were not very far from the centre of the glade by now. Although the growth beneath these tall trees was very different from the brush we had encountered the previous day, here and there where the trees thinned there were small dense patches of the same thorny creepers, and it was in one of these that we expected the leopard to lie up.

We had just started moving on when there was a rustling high overhead in the tree-tops and we instantly froze. Dassie looked up over his shoulder, but when the cause of the disturbance turned out to be a troop of monkeys, he immediately lowered his head to pick up the spoor again. The interest the monkeys had showed in us made us feel reasonably sure that the leopard could not be anywhere near by, but no sooner had we come to this conclusion than Eric stopped me again and said under his breath, 'I am not so sure. Perhaps he is hidden in one of these patches of creeper where they can't spot him.' However, as Dassie was following the spoor determinedly, we decided that the best we could do was to watch him carefully, because he would certainly bristle and stop if we got to within a hundred yards of the leopard, as he had done on several occasions when we were after lynxes in the Free State. At the same time we held him firmly in leash, since we knew that if there was only one dog he could not possibly escape the lightning-like charge of a leopard. All we wanted of him was to lead us to the quarry.

And sure enough, we had gone about a hundred yards farther, and were approaching a particularly dense patch of vines, when Dassie stopped suddenly and gave a suppressed and hardly audible snort, and bristled from tail to neck. There was a slight movement of air from the right so he tried to pull me to the left in order better to test it, and pinpoint the exact spot where the leopard was lying up, but I whispered a decided 'nee' under my breath.

We came to a dead stop, and I glanced at Eric and saw that he was tense with expectation. Then there was a rustling overhead, and looking up we saw a monkey who had presumably come to have a closer look at us, give a prodigious leap from one tree to another, and at the same moment there was a slight crash in the brake ahead of us, and we had a fleeting but clear glimpse of the leopard as it sailed over a dead branch and out of sight. We knew that he was clearing out and we hoped fervently that he would come within range of one of the guns; but we were closer to the edge of the wood than we had realized and the leopard's keen ears must have warned him where Pieter and Cronje sat waiting for him. The upshot was that he slipped past them so silently that they remained unaware of him.

We went out and joined them and as soon as the beaters had caught up with us we once more followed Dassie, and on the fresh spoor it was all we could do to keep up with him. As we climbed higher up the mountain slope the open stretches between the clumps of forest were becoming narrower, so we decided to keep Dassie on the leash, but to loose the other dogs in the hopes that the leopard might take to a tree if he found himself surrounded by a number of them. But as soon as they got the fresh scent most of them bristled, stuck their tails between their hind legs, and retreated behind us. Only three took up the spoor and raced after the marauder. We followed them as far as we could and soon we heard by their furious barking that the leopard was at bay. Then, when we were still about fifty yards off, there was a yelp of pain, and almost immediately two dogs with tails between their legs dashed towards us. All was quiet, and we advanced with the utmost caution, and before long we stumbled on the body of the missing dog. The leopard must have leapt down on him from a tree for except for a bite on his neck we could see no scratch on him.

We were now no longer pursuing a fleeing animal, but up against a harried leopard that had tasted blood—one of the most dangerous of all animals. All the dogs but Dassie had fled, and we dared not endanger the lives of the natives by asking them to try and drive out an angry leopard in such cover. And so after weighing the pros and cons we decided that the four of us and Dassie should make one more attempt to settle accounts with the marauder.

The spoor now led straight up towards the cliffs at the top of the mountain, passing through the larger patches of forest, and bypassing the smaller ones, till we found ourselves in a maze of tumbled rocks and tangled vegetation beneath overhanging cliffs. It would have been madness to attempt to scale them, and we decided to go no further. We had reached a small clearing where there would have been barely enough room for us to stretch out and relax had we wished to. A high krans towered above us, festooned with clinging creepers that half hid a ledge of rock to the right, and below this there was a deep and rocky chasm dividing it from the lower ground. Dassie was very restless and showed every sign of scenting the leopard close at hand, and as he sniffed he kept looking upwards. But we felt it would be suicidal to attempt to go any further, though out of sheer habit we all still spoke in whispers, and made every effort not even to break a twig.

Then, as someone struck a match there was a slight rustle from above and a few pebbles and some loose earth and dry leaves fell down. Eric's face lighted up. 'He is there,' he said. 'Fire a shot to the right. He'll have to clear the chasm and escape to the left. We'll try and have a snap shot at him if he shows himself.' I waited just until Eric, Cronje and Pieter stood at the ready and then I fired into the creeper-covered ledge. A yellowish streak shot out and sailed over the chasm in a graceful curve; but the sights of three guns were following its line of flight, and as the animal's front feet touched the opposite krans there was a volley and a heavy body disappeared into the chasm, riddled by bullets. Splashes of blood showed where it had struck against the rocks as it fell into the dark rift from which we knew it would be impossible to retrieve it.

And now Dassie was set free from the restraining leash. He knew that the leopard was dead and he trotted cheerfully down the mountain just ahead of us.

Dassie and the Bushpig

THE NEXT DAY I was alone on the farm except for a few domestic servants. Our negotiations with the timber company for the removal of the eucalyptus trees had been unsuccessful, so we were considering boring for water. There was the possibility too that we might be able to pipe the water of a perennial spring in a beautiful kloof, below which there were many acres of deep, rich soil.

I had to return to the Free State in less than a month, and as there was still a lot to be seen to, I completely abandoned the idea of trying to reduce the pigs or scaring them off. Dassie was enjoying a rest after the two strenuous days he had just had, and besides he was limping as the result of several thorns I had not been able to remove. But by the end of the week he was himself again and was following me everywhere and giving every indication that he was thoroughly tired of doing nothing. He never let me out of his sight for a moment, and he would crouch with his head resting on his forepaws watching every movement, and waiting for me to put on my old felt hat or take up a gun. And every now and then he would sidle up and tilt at a hand with his cold nose, which was his way of saying, 'Come along! Why waste precious time.'

Whenever we were short of meat, and I was obliged to go out after pheasant, guinea-fowl or duiker, his joy knew no bounds. I purposely avoided the deeper kloofs where we might encounter pig or bushbuck, and hugged the foot of the mountain where smaller game could always be found.

About two weeks had passed when one hot night the air was so oppressive that I opened the door of the rondavel in which I slept and placed the coat on which Dassie slept near the entrance so that no snake or other intruder should be able to get in. It must have been about ten o'clock and I was still awake when I heard a slight noise, and looking up I saw Dassie moving slowly out into the moonlight. About half an hour passed and he did not return. I began to wonder what he was up to, and I was just about to go out and investigate when I heard him barking about three hundred yards away on the slope below the homestead. Listening intently I heard the barking change into those quickly reiterated half yelps he was in the habit of making when chasing anything.

Whatever he was after was making towards the kloofs on the higher slopes, and to say that I was perturbed was to put it mildly. Going after porcupines or lynxes as he had done in the Free State in country he had known since he was a puppy was one thing; but to be venturing out alone in this difficult wilderness to run on the spoor of one of its dangerous inhabitants was quite another.

I hurriedly put on my shirt, trousers and shoes, and seizing the shot gun and a torch I hastened in the direction he had taken. The moon was almost at the full and for the first hundred yards or so I was going across fairly open ground. In fact I remember thinking that I might as well have left the torch behind. Then I stopped to listen and I could tell that whatever

Dassie was after was at bay and had probably turned to fight. His barking came from the direction of the deep kloof beyond the first ridge, and to try and barge my way straight through would have been sheer madness. Fortunately I remembered that there was a disused and by now hardly discernible native footpath leading up to the top of the kloof, from where I should probably be within two or three hundred yards of the fight. I found it and as I began to follow it, I saw that I had cause to bless the moment I had seized the torch. Though bushpig and bushbuck had taken to the track it was so overgrown in places, and so blocked by dead trees that had fallen across it that I could never have picked my way without the light. The path seemed endless but when at last I got to the top of the intervening ridge, I heard Dassie's bark, and at any rate I knew that he was still alive. I had now to descend into the trees and brush of the deep kloof where the leaves shut out most of the moonlight, and I was once again dependent on the torch. As I flashed it down the steep slope, the light suddenly caught two pairs of eyes, one green and the other reddish, and I have no recollection of how I got through the tangle after that. All I knew was that my presence would encourage Dassie to attack quite recklessly, and I could tell from the grunts that he was fighting a bushpig.

The trees were sparser here, and I could see the two of them dimly in the moonlight. Dassie was hanging on to one of the pig's hind legs, when it suddenly swung round, lifting him off his feet. His hold parted and the pig made a vicious sideways jab at him, but thanks to the violence with which he had been flung off, its tusk just grazed his back. Dassie retreated towards me with the pig in pursuit, and before I knew where I was a terrific bump sent me tumbling backwards into a clump of thorns. When I picked myself up I found that I was still holding the gun, but the torch was gone.

Dassie was once more hanging on to a hind leg, and I lifted my gun. I was only about five yards from the pig, but it was impossible to align the sights in that uncertain light, so I fired point blank. The pig dropped out of sight, but when I heard Dassie working off his anger by tugging at it with might and main, I knew it was dead. It was the luckiest shot of my life, for not only was there hardly any light, but I had hurt a leg in the fall, and was decidedly shaky on the other. Casting about I found that the torch was still intact, and warily and painfully I approached the spot where Dassie was grunting and growling. The shot gun fired at such close range had made a gaping hole in the pig's head.

But by now I could think of nothing but to get home as quickly as possible. I found to my relief that though my trousers had been ripped open from the knee to the middle of the thigh, I had suffered no other injury than a severe bump; so severe indeed that I found later that a ligament had been torn. A depression at that spot will always remain to remind me of an exciting adventure. Early the next day Jan and a number of boys, with Dassie leading them, went to bring in the bushpig.

For two weeks I hobbled about with a stiff leg, and I was constantly worried lest Dassie should try to carry on his feud with the pigs. I knew that it was luck as much as ability that had thus far helped him to escape with his life. So to avoid further encounters, especially as my leg made it impossible for me to help him, I saw to it that our rondavel door remained closed during the hours of darkness.

The end of Dassie

THE DAY CAME when my work on the farm was finished and one glorious morning as the sun rose over the eastern ranges I said goodbye to Eric and the family, and Dassie and I started on our long journey southwards towards the Free State. The beautiful hills and mountains of Modjadje gradually faded from our view, but my regrets were lessened by the prospect of seeing again the koppies and endless grassy flats of the Free State where I was born and bred. Now and then Dassie who was in the back of the car would stand up and rest his forepaws on top of the front seat, lean against my shoulder and touch my ear with his cold nose—all this to elicit a little friendly conversation. No one else would have understood us, but to Dassie it was completely satisfying and after a little he would sink back to settle on his old coat with a groan of contentment.

At last in the late afternoon we turned away to the east on the road that leads to Rooiwal, the home of the Van der Merwes, where I intended staying over for a few days' fishing before we resumed the journey to Bloemfontein. And so the next afternoon found Dassie and me on the banks of the Rhenoster River, close to the railway bridge.

To reach the spot I had in view we had to cross the bridge and go a few hundred yards upstream, leaving the car on the near side. Carrying over our stuff was no easy matter as the footplates alongside the rails were narrow and slippery, and one false step would have meant a fall of forty or fifty feet on to jagged rocks and cement blocks below. As we were to spend the night at the river there was too much in the way of fishing gear, food and bedding to be carried over in one journey; but at last we could settle down and were ready for our afternoon and night's sport.

As the sun was setting I went back to see if all was well at the car. From our side of the bridge I noticed a suspicious looking character hanging around and peering into it, so I gave Dassie the command '*kar toe* (to the car)'. He at once crossed the bridge and barking furiously rushed up to the stranger, who slunk off into the mimosa patch on the bank. That night the fish were greedily on the bite and I forgot about the car; but before going to sleep I made one more trip to see that everything was in order. After that I drowsed and though trains were passing and repassing I took very little notice, and the whistling of the engines hardly penetrated my consciousness. But I could not quite banish from my mind the suspicious looking stranger, and at about twelve o'clock I told Dassie to go the car again. He returned in less than half an hour and by his manner I felt certain that all was well and I fell asleep again. At about two o'clock in the morning I woke and found that he was not with me. This did not, however, surprise me as he had got into the habit of returning to the car at almost regular intervals whenever we slept away from it. Not long after I hooked a really large fish, but it took the line round an obstruction and in the end I was forced to use so much tension that it snapped. I was all eagerness then to hook another such big fellow and thought no more of sleeping.

The sun was about to rise when I suddenly realized that the dog had not yet returned, and I became very uneasy, for Dassie had never stayed away like that before. As quickly as I could I cleared the bank, and went back to look for him. As I was crossing the bridge my eyes fell on a blotch of blood on one of the footplates. I stopped as if shot, unable to think. Then as the numbness passed from my mind, I was afraid to look over the rails at the jagged rocks below. But I knew now that Dassie must have been killed by a passing train, and flung off the line by the cowcatcher. At last I bent to look over the side, and there in a sandy patch between two cement blocks lay Dassie, exactly as I had seen him so many times lying on his side on the clean sands of the Modder river.

Presently I found myself standing over his body. The cowcatcher had caught him in the middle of the forehead and must have caused instant death, for which even then I was deeply thankful. Except for his head injury he was untouched. What had probably happened was that he was blinded by the headlights of an engine when he was on the bridge, returning from an inspection of the car.

A native was speaking to me from the bridge above and I asked him to help me. We carried him to level ground above the bank, and the native who worked at the farmhouse close by brought a spade and pickaxe. We dug deep, and laid dry grass below and above him so that the cold bare earth should not touch him. The man then helped me to carry my things back to the car, while I moved along as one in a dream; and the drive back to the farm is a blank. The people there, all friends of Dassie's, were very kind.

I left early the next day on my way back to Bloemfontein. Several times out of sheer habit I looked round. The old coat was still there in its place near the back window, and I found it hard to realize that I should not again feel him lean against me or hear his little groan of contentment as he sank back.

At last I reached home, and at the gate my eyes lighted on the little patch of lawn where Dassie used to await my homecoming. But it is fitting that he should have found a last resting place on the banks of a river, beneath warm suns and star-studded skies, where the wind sighs through the mimosas as the sky reddens in the east.